PROXIES

PROXIES

Essays Near Knowing

_____

{ *a reckoning* }

Brian Blanchfield

NIGHTBOAT BOOKS

NEW YORK

© 2016 Brian Blanchfield

Printed in the United States

ISBN 978-1-937658-45-8

Design and typesetting by Mary Austin Speaker

Text set in Bembo

Cataloging-in-publication data is available from the Library of Congress.

This is a work of literary nonfiction in which there are accounts of lived experience. The author has tried to recreate events and conversations from his memories of them. Some names and identifying details have been changed to protect the privacy of individuals.

Distributed by the University Press of New England

One Court Street

Lebanon, NH 03766

www.upne.com

Nightboat Books

New York

www.nightboat.org

[contents]

[A Note]

At the end of this book there is a rolling endnote called "Correction." It sets right much—almost certainly not all—of what between here and there I get wrong. It runs to twenty-one pages. It may still be running.

Susceptibility to error is a hazard inherent to *Proxies*. From the beginning (the first of these single-subject essays were written in 2009 and the majority were written in the years 2013–15), I decided on a total suppression of recourse to other authoritative sources. I wrote these essays with the internet off. I determined not to review again the books and other works I consulted in memory, and I did not stop thinking through the subject at hand to verify assertions or ground speculation or firm up approximations. *Que sais-je?*, Montaigne asked his library shelves one day late in the sixteenth century, and increasingly that seems a good start.

Having determined that this would be unresearched essaying, analytic but nonacademic, I was almost immediately drawn to a second constraint—or, better, invitation: to stay with the subject until it gives onto an area of personal uneasiness, a site of vulnerability, and keep unpacking from there. The formula I found for titling the individual essays was generated very early on, to operate this request of self. Clumsy as it may be, I claim as part of a personal sortilege a devotion to the words I had bannered across the top of each new developing piece, an invocation of sorts, a ritual. *Permitting shame, error and guilt...*

Proxies changed as I changed. The uniformity of this repeatable experiment, as described, ended up providing a frame for variation, expansion over time. I've kept the essays in the order I wrote them, more or less—whatever development can be tracked may correspond to what might be called a self. They are not the same thing. This is a book braver than I am.

A proxy in one sense is a position: a stand-in, an agent, an avatar, a functionary, and I am acquainted with the office. I have been stepson, house sitter, replacement faculty, liaison, trustee, interim director, secretary, adjunct, sub, temp, warm body, and for a short while acting editor of *The Prostate*—I still have the letterhead). *Whose office is this?* is a deputy's question to answer, a tricky one, and also *On whose behalf; on what authority do you have it?*

In sciences I think *proxy* additionally expresses a kind of concession to imprecision, a failure. It's the word for a subject you choose to study to produce data that can *approximate* the data you'd get from the actual, desired subject, if it were not prohibitively hard to apprehend.

If that's not entirely accurate, it's close.

PROXIES

On Owls

Permitting Shame, Error and Guilt, Myself the Single Source

Finally I went, after many years of wanting to—of telling people about the place—at age twenty-one or so, to the raptor center outside Charlotte, my hometown, on a date, with a boy, the second boy I ever slept with. Had I waited for the boy love phase of my life to realize? He had an interest in falconry, which conjoined with his collector's interest in swords and scabbards, as anyone who entered his bedroom on Ideal Way could readily discern. I met him surreptitiously at my stepfather's fiftieth birthday dinner (he was the waiter) and would drive down from Chapel Hill to be with him, a year or two younger than I. I barely knew what I wanted from him, beyond the conspiratorial audacity of his returned interest when I trailed him to the parking lot. I had loved the way he looked at me and received the thread of challenge in the eyes. I remember there were bricks arranged in a sunburst around a sort of monument in the middle of the raptor center, which was mostly outdoors (contrary to my expectations), and they were named for donors whose moderate interest in and support for birds of prey could be immortalized. One brick one donor: I was so late to the metaphor I appreciated it. It was 1995. I bought someone a brick for a gift but I can't remember who. It wasn't Greg, I don't think. Their captivity was mostly rehabilitative—the large, clean, wooded, lidded cages were full of injured birds, falcons the smallest and commonest. I'm sure there was an owl. Time was what they needed. Time was what needed doing.

If there was an owl, it was still. Owls are best known to me by their frightening fixity. Why is a still thing upsetting? Because it might move. Also, iconographically—that is, reductively, in caricature—owls have a concentricity about their feathery faces, circles around the circles of their eyes. I wrote a poem about not sleeping with a man who had given me ecstasy once, about putting my pants on in the east Manhattan morning, and I used the term *little professor* in it, in caricature. Little Professor is a children's game with an owl as its logo, plastic and circular and orange like the Seventies.

"The Owl in the Sarcophagus" is a poem by Wallace Stevens that I have read but cannot remember well, probably not much about either an owl or a sarcophagus, though in its title it draws the ready sensation of a fable or else a science fiction story. The titular owl fits into the sarcophagus, and sarcophagus like geophagy may contain the root of the word to eat and there is a sense that the sarcophagus—capable presumably of surrounding or containing the owl—may also devour it. A sarcophagus seems to me a better word for a cocoon, but it is a coffin. The owl is alone, in the sarcophagus, and alone in Stevens, where there are many birds, all of whom appear in flocks or in patchy families, gathering of a sudden with their southern color in an otherwise bare northern tree, changing it with a flourish, in a flourish by which Stevens often means powers of attention or imagination. An owl has a different kind of attention than Stevens has. She will not break it after boredom comes. An owl does not bore, as long as it lives.

The frightening owl my mother sends in a picture text on her camera phone seems impossibly large and threatening, training its stare at first my mother and then me. The note she writes says "it let me get within five feet." Was she seeking its yellow-eyed counsel? When I finally write back I ask about its wingspan, because I suppose I want to imagine the moment after its permission is withdrawn, I want to imagine this bird flown.

On Completism

Permitting Shame, Error and Guilt, Myself the Single Source

My ex-boyfriend Doug uses the word in describing himself, completist, the way I used to and still sometimes call myself a revivalist or a scopophilic, for me because I like a summarial word that takes care of identity, subsuming identity into character, as my friend Aaron might say—though often I misconstrue what Aaron might say on the subject of character—making myself a member or even an exemplar of a type. There's a kind of joke in it on complexity—I reduce myself to a kind, and because my true nature is contrarianism (I am a contrarian, but not merely a contrarian, for again I am additionally a complexifier) and I bristle at definitive limits, it is perverse I should be drawn to the elegance of category: one goes into one once, no remainder on the roof. I typify scopophilia because I like to watch something in secret, and I might leave it at that, painful (and therefore pleasurable) as it is not to modify or complicate that appraisal. Doug is a completist, he will say, to anyone reviewing his cd collection—he has all the New Order albums, and is collecting everything recorded at Factory Records, Manchester. He keeps together the stubs of each month's power, phone, and Direct TV bills, respectively; he has a box of years of *Interview* magazine, a collection which Warhol would surely have commended and indeed anticipated.

Completism has this to do with death or the death drive. Life is in the commonest measure a duration, experientially incremental and final only when finished, and it is easy to be persuaded by Barbara Hernnstein-Smith or Jean Baudrillard or someone who has done the reasoning to see matters of aesthetics as appreciation of part-whole relations, the analogy an easy one, but real I suppose. The completist, upon obtaining the Mike Schmidt third baseman card, may claim then to have in his collection the entire set of 1981 Philadelphia Phillies player trading cards. The achievement therein is that a comprehensive perspective has been prepared, a panorama in miniature, a panorama ne plus ultra. The completist can see all at once the entirety of the 1981 Philadelphia Phillies club and so has looked upon his own death. That is, he has done the advance work sufficiently to pull out widely enough to see the thing in whole. He even has the manager's card, Sparky Anderson or Whitey Herzog, and can review the full measure of the set, soup to nuts.

The completist's real joy comes in the ability to withdraw one member of the set and behold it singly, snugly comforted by the comprehension that it has a place in the lineup, a positional belonging. It oscillates in isolation between object and component, and the overseeing consciousness to whom this is true rests confident in the knowledge that this cannot be disputed. I have used the word *overseeing*, and the word *panorama*, and certainly the completist is a god, a just and benign one, since his plenary dominion wants nothing.

My failure continually to complete anything is not, as logic may indicate, a fear of death, but—to the contrary—a fear of life. When I back away from a poem I back away at that exceptional moment it begins to come together under my attentions and other slants of propitious light. The deepest breakthrough I have experienced thus far with Emery Jones, LCPC, of Missoula, Montana, is that when I cried so much as a child, nearly daily until fourth grade, it was often because I had been touched by something or demanded by something and had felt the sudden reality of my presence and then the deep shame—particularly in an embrace with a kind or alarmed adult—that theretofore I had been something (and on purpose, by choice), something other than alive.

On Sardines

Permitting Shame, Error and Guilt, Myself the Single Source

Sardines is or was a hiding game that accommodates multiple players and represents a significant improvement on hide-and-seek—or, rather a developmental advancement—as it introduces the social and psychosexual into the foundational game of independence rehearsal whose basic rudiments are absence, reassurance, detection, and self-concealment. The child who experiences in hide-and-seek the rueful pleasure of empathic superimposition ("she will never find me here") is a candidate for Sardines. Sardines builds into the familiar format the stirring new elements of conspiracy, refuge, betrayal, gratification deferral, cultural assimilation, and sustained bodily contact.

One person hides and everyone else, each member of the search party, is It, a party whose number dwindles as, upon discovery of the chosen hiding place, a searcher suppresses any paroxysm of triumph and covertly joins the hidden party, cramming himself silently into the closet or crawlspace, in effect turncoating his detective affiliation to steal away for safe haven, to become a refugee among refugees. The shared hideout toward the end of a round of Sardines is a squirming mass of maximally compressed, clinging bodies in the dark trying not to laugh or breathe audibly until the final discovery is made and the game has its villainous loser, on whom the constriction of frozen postures and half erections and self-estimations and collective suspense outpours and unburdens itself, spilling and showering around him the loud relief—real for some and feigned by others—of unstrung individualities distinct again and reviewing comparatively their dismay. It is a game of early adolescence.

Ordained confinement wherein embrace is organized as a situational necessity is recognizably the ground floor of my erotic imagination. My early fantasies and even dreams were perforce arrangements of closeness with boys, ingenious scenarios that late cold-war tropes helped to prepare: root cellars during a tornado scare, bomb shelters, prisoners' quarters, deep dry wells, or dens within caves demanded that another haplessly subterranean boy whose form I could barely make out in the pitch black must stand or lie squarely against me. Endless stimulation in the *fort-da* wiggle room between speculation and the highly conditional permission to touch: Does he feel what I feel? and then, We have no choice, we have to be like this. Experience finally suggested that unconscious invention of such imperatives is common within culturally abhorrent sexuality. In the homoerotic film *Brothers of the Head*, by Lou Pepe and Keith Fulton, the metaphor is precisely exteriorized: conjoined twins inseparable at the torso have grown into young adulthood in early Eighties downtrodden industrial England and fashion themselves as a punk duo, shirtless and indignant onstage and with the prurient press, wrapping their arms around one another, turning from the spotlights so that the mouth of one is ever whispering distance from the ear of the other, because (what if, so what) they have to.

"Because we have to" is a construct different from the fresh "because we can" punchline of sexual liberation. It values freedom differently, and is implicitly defensive, defensible. The identity-political same-sex Eighties, backing itself into the corner of legitimacy, begs the pardon of its ruling fathers by a civil means. It happened within each body: think of each body listening, at the cultural culmination of confinement erotics in the Reagan-Thatcher era, the famous double live album *101* by industrial band Depeche Mode, drenchingly and reverberantly sinister—replete with sounds of hydraulic releases, chain pulleys, and vise cranks—when the chamber endgame atmosphere is distilled for the ballad "Somebody," which details a fantasy of complete intimacy with some specular somebody imaginable and fully other, and which ends, "In a place like this, I'll get away with it." The rapt crowd is thick, aroused, blandished, sanctioned, beside themselves before the lickerish bouquet.

On Br'er Rabbit

Permitting Shame, Error and Guilt, Myself the Single Source

Br'er was a trouble word in early 1980s North Carolina, for a working class white boy who knew from picture books what rabbits and foxes and bears were, who knew too that "brother" was a nonfamilial term belonging to male junior members not yet "elder" in the church, but who had problems pronouncing his r's, even the antagonizing ones in his own name and home, Brian Overby of Rural Hall. I troubled, too, over what the word indicated and how it functioned, since it was suggestive of a name and thereby in a different category, I had imputed, from words with meanings you could ask for, but had none of the singularity of a name—like Friar Tuck, I would've said—specific to one person alone; it was given to Rabbit and Fox and Bear alike. If it was a rank, like deputy, then it begged more questions, as to why Br'er Bear or Br'er Fox had license to discipline Br'er Rabbit in the stories. *Br'er* was a word I grouped by appearance and sound with *ne'er* and *where'er* from the Old School Hymnal we sang from in church and it shared therefore a whiff of vinegary bygones and preternatural power I had learned (by transgressing the sacrosanct) to leave be. If pressed, I might have estimated that "br'er" was an alternate presentation of the briars Rabbit made his home, but I also suspected it indicated a special kind (that is, qualitatively different from the familiar species) of rabbit, bear, and fox, an inversion somehow of those creatures—like werewolves.

Otherness was, of course—ever since their white and self-appointed amanuensis Joel Chandler Harris had copied and popularized the African trickster narratives that had survived among enslaved populations in Georgia—as inseparable from the Uncle Remus stories as Br'er Rabbit's fists were from the Tar Baby. But, by the time I was considering them, their alterity had been compounded by a century more of racism and contentious integration to the degree that, somewhat early on, I understood the lesson of that particular fable to be: Engagement of the latent problem—on the grounds that even its mute presence disturbs you—will only prove your sticky complicitness in the trouble. It was reasonably a parable about the races in the South after slavery, divisive but unstable, as several things complicated the fashion in which, for generations, white children were supposed to be interpellated by Uncle Remus, listening at his feet. For one, it was easy to appreciate that *tar baby* had become a slur (even more insidious, because more comprehensible, than *picaninny*, still prevalent in my childhood) before ever reading the story, and the key question was whether Br'er Rabbit was black—since his inextricability from the form of the tar baby figure would logically have suggested he was white—whether Rabbit and Bear and Fox were each black, all black, that is, whether "br'er" meant black, a question I worked over and did not ask.

The "briar patch," too, as cultural meme, history made unsteady, for while it conveys admiration of wiliness and reverse psychology, its other suggestion is perilous: that discipline founders either when it aims to, or else when it fails to, select the captive's nightmare experience. I had been pitched into the briar patch, it was acknowledged, whenever my punishment was solitude, to which I was happily accustomed ("I live here!" was the episode's conclusion), concluding too the conscious performance of the parent-captor as bad disciplinarian, or good master. "That's mighty white of you," my mother might say to my father when he offered to stack his plate and saucer but not to take them to the sink or wash them. Subtending familial relationships in Southern white households then with narrow perspectives, weakened heritage, and no initiative beyond economic betterment was the master-servant template, demanding allegiance and compliance, expecting parry and subterfuge, and rehearsing moreover Old South subject positions, casually racist in their ventriloquism and chilling anachronism.

Kenny Stewart, my neighbor, an older boy whom I adulated at age seven or eight, was the first person ever to ask me whether I was a Christian. I can remember having no response, even as he elaborated his query, ashamed not to know that a Primitive Baptist *was* a Christian. His mother, who agreed to look after me afternoons, instructed me to say "urinate" when I needed to pee, and brought me along for her children's piano lessons, horseback riding lessons, and even their famous family reunions, where I was the only white kid running around Freedom Park. It was this family, whose healthy civility afforded a place for me, who brought my identities out, who brought me up in the contrastive open, where I might draw the line for myself later, not long after, when my uncle introduced me to another kind like him as a "good ol' boy" and I knew the voucher was as bogus as the impunity it was meant to purchase, even if I stood in the new difference mute as a tar doll.

On Foot Washing

Permitting Shame, Error and Guilt, Myself the Single Source

Foot washing is a sacrament in Protestant orders that understand the Bible as the word of God, including the Old Particular Baptists and the Primitive Baptists, especially in the Piedmont and Appalachian regions from Pennsylvania to Georgia. In the Primitive Baptist churches I grew up in, the ritual was part of an annual communion. After a short sermon or reading from scripture—I think there is a story in which Christ humbles himself to wash the feet even of the apostles who would soon betray him and enjoins others to such humility—the members of the church would rise to sing hymns, called out by title or hymnal page number, and a procession would begin in an orderly fashion such that, sister with sister, and brother with brother, a pair would form and a wash basin would be chosen to fill with warm water. With two small white towels the partners would sit on and kneel before the front pew and alternate soaping and rinsing the feet of the other. It was touching to watch an elder and younger man exchange the service, lean and muscular, gnarly and horned. Maybe ten basins were in use at a time, and everyone else kept up the singing while the pair worked silently. I sang the lyrics of "Palms of Victory" or "Come Unto Me," watching every grimace and blush on my mother's face with her slender feet in the old woman's hands the last time. A thirteen year-old knows his single mother's foot. *An 8½ narrow*: back when a Naturalizer salesman would bring his shoehorn and ramp-stool over to straddle his customer's fitting.

To wash one's own feet independent of the rest of the body, and even to wash the feet of others, was not an unusual act in the time and place Jesus Christ lived, in an economy of hospitality,

Greek in origin. He and his friends wore sandals, of course, and customarily the feet were the most unclean part of anyone entering a home, particularly travelers. Was that the function of the first foyer, the anteroom? Odysseus, dressed as the beggar back at Ithaca, was recognized by the scar on his leg when the old nurse was cleaning his feet. A warm foot bath was a welcome, and for a friend to give one to a fellow friend was perhaps a tenderness. Reciprocity was at the heart of it. Not to return the favor was to upset a balance. It may well be that, originally, "the shoe was on the other foot" when an erstwhile guest held his former host's upon repayment of a visit. Somewhere Guy Davenport must have an annotated bibliography on the topic, tracking it homosocially through art and literature.

In Greek drama it was even more honorable to wash a horrible foot, a putrid foot. In *Philoctetes*, the ogre has been exiled on his island on account of a deception rooted in foot disgust. His fellow sailors led their wounded, festering compatriot ashore and sneaked back to the boat slip without him, unable any longer to abide the smell of his rank, diseased, accursed foot. But the play concerns a second deception in which a young honorable man is enlisted, by Odysseus, to gain Philoctetes' trust, to hear his laments and sympathize, to enter his cave and tolerate the stench—and then snatch the ogre's magic bow when he is seized again predictably by foot pain. Because the young man's sympathy is real, his guile is tested. Nonetheless he executes the plan and procures the treasured bow for Odysseus in the wings. It is for Philoctetes as though the first betrayal was reopened. Whatever psychic detachment from his own extremity he had managed is annihilated. His relationship with his own living rot, we know then, will only grow more shameful. And Odysseus, elsewhere the revenant hero, messiah incognito, is here a craven opportunist, whose villainy, equally, is detachment from shame.

When my stepfather Frank, in a torrent of spite and fury, humiliates my mother in the company of family or friends, over dinner or in his own hospital room, as he does regularly, relentlessly, set off by her miscomprehension of something or an oversight he has discovered, the room is stunned, shaken. There is nothing like it. Mortification is arresting for everyone present. However nefarious or admirable his other dealings may have been, the great disgrace of his life will have been his terrorism of the one devoted to him. The lasting shame of mine was enduring it by detaching from it. I left when I was seventeen, five years into their marriage, and I visit as seldom as I feel I can.

Frank has had, for five or six years now, a chronic wound on the sole of his right foot, a condition not uncommon to advanced type 2 diabetics like himself. Bones in his feet are gradually crumbling and splaying, and abrasions form. Charcot Syndrome. Because of the related impaired circulation and complete localized nerve loss, there is no pain, but there is constant danger of necrosis and toxic shock. The wound on his sole has intermittently wept and cracked and granulated for years, but never closed, despite a number of stimulative water and pressure and debridement treatments, and its inability to heal is the single reason he has been prohibited the kidney transplant for which he arranged a donor long ago but for which he would need to be infection-free during post-operative immunosuppresion therapy. The aperture of his wound has varied from dime to half-dollar size and I have seen it three or four inches deep. Even then, it was frightfully clean, like a throat.

My mother cleans it, every evening, after dinner, after the dishes. She has a kit, a kind of carpet bag, with gloves and sprays and brushes and ointments and individually wrapped antiseptic wipes. He lifts his heavy leg to the butcher block table in their kitchen, and her movements are quicker and rougher than you might imagine, though her concentration is intense. She wipes the gullet of it, and the rim, she gets it to granulate. After twenty-five years of marriage she knows this part of his body best. He hasn't ever really seen it. Often, during, feeling nothing, he watches television.

On Propositionizing

Permitting Shame, Error and Guilt, Myself the Single Source

When Helen Keller returns from the wellhouse with Miss Sullivan, she resists her teacher's escort and runs ahead to the house in my mind's eye, on bare, mosquito-bitten eleven-year-old legs, her hair a mess, in the hot thick summer of 1870s Tuscumbia, Alabama. She is euphoric. The most crucial event in her life had just happened. Or was still happening, revealing itself, like a slow burst, a bloom. Eleanor Wilner has a poem about the morning, a poem that ought to be called "Openness Happens in the Midst of Being" though that is the title of a Norman Dubie poem that seeks to evoke something of Heidegger and depends like a lot of those wry male domestic poems of the Seventies on the unlikeliness of the allusion, since it is about a couple watching a storm coming on, a deer crossing a lawn. Keller's experience seems categorically one in which, in Heideggerian terms, she is "thrown" into being. Walker Percy goes so far, in an essay called "The Delta Factor," to suggest that what happened in the wellhouse and for the rest of that day is that Helen Keller *became* a human being. The event began this way: in an instant, after months, she was able to comprehend that w-a-t-e-r, the *word* traced by Miss Sullivan in her one hand, *was* in some sense water the *substance*, pouring over her other. An imputed relation was hers to make. Had been an animal, became a human being. Had been an organism whose responses to stimuli could be observed; became an autocratic, creative, complex person capable of abstract thought, capable, in language, of propositionizing. The key component of language acquisition.

When I tell him what this one is about, my boyfriend John raises his eyebrows to ask if I mean propositioning. I know; it seems like there should be a better noun form. I think even in Roman Jakobson it's a term revived from farther back. It may be the whole concept is in disfavor, like ontogeny recapitulating phylogeny, like Heideggerian ontology. It's structural: the opposite of apposition in speech, I think; a proposition *says something about something.*

Percy's essay about language and its relationship to consciousness pays close attention to the way Keller explains her day in *The Story of My Life,* which she wrote when she was in her thirties. When she burst into the house, she was, she says, alive with the realization that all things and people had names, equivalences in language: sister, teacher, spoon, cat, doll. The doll she had earlier thrown in a tantrum she now held like a treasure, and was sorry for what she had done. She says that the knowledge she attained that day was discovery, but felt more like remembering, recapturing something that had been in oblivion before. *Sorry for what she had done,* bespeaking the new valuation of doll now that it had a tag by which she could retrieve it, is interesting, but sounds fishily pious, mixed in with shame at one's own behavior, and is likely the effect of Christian moralism, which in both her home and the Perkins School was doctrine. But, *discovering as though remembering*: that sounds spiritual rather than religious. It sounds Heideggerian. What Helen Keller gained was not the mere equivalence of names to objects and persons (and later concepts and states and actions); it was the power the other languaged humans have—to propose relationships among things, to formulate about things, to recast them; and the things themselves need not even be present. *A spoon emerges from water with water in it. The doll that teacher loved Helen shall hide and apologize. Quiet and clean are sisters.* This is propositionizing, in linguistics. This is the productivity of language, as Noam Chomsky called it, singularly human. This may be what explains the relatively rapid major increase in brain size and neural demand in early hominids two million years ago.

This is in language what Donald Winnicott insisted remain free in childhood play, our remake of our surroundings, our exercise of independence. This is what Aristotle mistrusted in poets, makers; we cannot leave things alone. We say what we like. There is a given world and then most of us graduate into a second given, an abstract realm where all of the entities of the given world are players that we can bring into transactive arrangements in sentences, by their names. Standing to reason is only one position. That was a proposition.

The upshot of Helen Keller's account and the reason I have taught the long Percy essay four or five times at the beginning of poetry courses even though it makes no mention of poetry is that Helen—who writes that in her crib that night she was wakeful, alive with possibility for the first time—had been altered constitutively by the ability to put words into play. So have we all been. Keller's developmental passage into the propositionizing phase is uniquely accelerated (a prolepsis in arrears) and isolable. What do we mean when we say she "comes into her own?" How is it we each understand exactly what that means? To arrive anew into one's birthright, one's selfhood? Roland Barthes uses nearly the same quivering expression as Keller, writing about the pleasure of choosing a word, not for its fitness or this or that sonorous or rich quality but for its "vibrating" potential, a "future praxis," its readiness to be "put into play" with others. I quote him directly on the syllabi, and Muriel Rukeyser, who says about one's first formative poem reading experience, connecting with its "multiple time sense," that it is discovery that feels like recognition, that such backward-reaching experiences of present time can even make one's mortality recede. To those I sometimes add Thomas Traherne's "The thought of the world whereby it is experienced is better than the world." And, maybe, six pillows rendered by Albrecht Dürer five hundred years ago and a map of seven days walking on Dartmoor by Richard Long. Together, they're like a personal sorcery. I suppose I am setting the stage for poetry to happen. Laying the propitious conditions for others to come into their own as though it were a return.

It can happen more than once, the return anew. Often you are permitted to return to a meadow. For instance, my boyfriend John is a poet, and I mark the exact moment I fell in love with him; it was a plunge I felt while reading a poem of his, a bracing little poem he had changed overnight, one of several in a manuscript. I had seen it the day before. We had had an exchange, and I made some remarks fielding and interpreting the associations and logic in the poem, in a shorthand we had developed in our exchange: "I like the strangeness of the question, Why are you always so vulnerable to be watched?...Wanting no one to find him is such an odd, sweet, macabre sort of overture. How does glitter help?...Love that higgledy mouth...Pick me up can also be as frequency and antennae do." It changed me to read what came back; I saw what he had done and how fast, how brilliant. For one thing, the material of my notes had been reconstituted in the poems, and he was showing me there. There was this "you" in the poems who was being readied to admit himself something, being admitted to readiness. He and the speaker were lit alike. "Like a / missing its shade / lamp is why you /...are so always / vulnerable / to watching." I recognized myself, in both senses. I was to myself re-known. "Show how you / are the first thermometer of the truck / flat sun, the jealous trees, the lemoning. Then / fuck on the side of the road." Was that propositionizing? It was like remembering what I needed to live, admitting what I wanted: to share the joy of remaking the world. Had been a reader; became an addressee. Coming into myself, what could I do? It was already happening. I was learning everything mine already to know. John was my student. We were graduating.

On the Locus Amoenus

Permitting Shame, Error and Guilt, Myself the Single Source

Latin. Right? Happy place. A pleasant place, a propitious place for happiness, luck, creativity, abundance of spirit to take hold. Does everyone have one? The locus amoenus is one of the early conventions of the pastoral mode, which is the oldest minor genre in poetry and lyric writing, and maybe the most mutable. In a certain light, Gwendolyn Brooks's urban Bronzeville poems from the Sixties were pastorals: linked persona poems whose dropped-in-on scenes together made up a village, a community; and in another light so is Rufus Wainwright's cover of The Beatles' "This Boy": nostalgic, plaintive, performing and lamenting the fungibility of men as love partners. "This Boy": it's the one that begins "That boy...isn't good for you." (He sings it with Sean Lennon, the slight one, at cross purposes.) Most commonly now we think of the pastoral as nature poetry or soft-focused naturalist writing, potentially embarrassing for its unproblematized birdsong and lilting reverie on the wonders of streams. But nature itself was in the work of Theocritus and later Virgil only a kind of stage, a theater for the idyll or eclogue or scene to begin.

The poem or songful story would be spoken by a "shepherd"— that is, by a young man who was amative and uninhibited, rascally, gracefully intelligent, highly literate, musical, fit, unself-conscious, curly-haired and beautiful, *and* the capable herder of livestock meanwhile. The early urban poet's ideal of the rural shepherd, goatherd, neatherd, or swain was implausible, a fantasy. That's who *spoke* the poem, which could be a number of things but was often an extrapolation of a detail in a myth known well by listeners. The listeners too were a fixed premise: fellow shepherds and lyrists who

23

were sometimes involved by name in the poem. What was it like for Herakles to leave his men and search frantically for his young, barefoot lover who had been drowned by river nymphs attracted to his beauty? Well, before I tell you, I must have led my sheep to pasture and found some shade, confident of their containment. It must be noontime, which is the most sempiternal of hours in the day. The sweet competitiveness of other shepherds who know my reputation as a poet and lover must be about me, electric. And, I must be in the right place. A clearing or a glade, a hillside outcropping of rounded rock one happens upon, with the long golden hair of the grasses matted and soft. The locus amoenus.

It is a reasonable question to ask, whether the poet is different from the person who writes the poems and pays the Comcast bill late again and gets balsamic dressing on the side and snaps at the customer service person at U-Haul headquarters. The philosopher and poet Allen Grossman makes the distinction between them and further suggests—best as I could tell and as well as I recall—that the poet (I believe he says the "poet in time") is contingent on the poem, is made the poet by the poem, each poem. A sort of separation happens perhaps. I think Grossman divides him up further and identifies, third, the lyric speaker as the default voice itself in a lyric poem, which in fact we do recognize immediately in poetry, the voice that is more overheard than heard. *Often I am permitted to return to a meadow.* If that spoken line were piped in through an intercom, you would still know right away it was poetry. *This is someone unnamed saying something to someone unnamed, either in a particular context or in the realm of forms, I am not him, and I want you to hear it.* Come into earshot. In what kind of place is all the hearing overhearing? The kind of place where all the looking is onlooking. The *locus amoenus.*

So, am I in a voice in a poem; or am I in a place from which I've prepared to speak; or have I situated someone other there, a figure, a projection, to speak, so to speak? More than a decade ago, after giving a reading, reading some of the early poems that went into my first book, I remember clearly a particular consternation someone felt and related to me. I think it was the following day. It was someone not especially familiar with poetry but someone who knew me well; I can't remember who. It's the kind of experience that repeats a half dozen times, in dreams too, until you sort of equip yourself for it. There is a question that is embarrassing, kind of flooring in its reasonableness. The question is easy but the answer is hard. (Isn't it always, about identity?) The person asks, maybe even works up the nerve to challenge: "But why does what you write not sound like how you talk?"

Why is poetry pretentious? Is that the question? Certainly to answer "Well, there I was speaking as my representative shepherd" doesn't help the cause. There are all kinds of ways to answer the question, including to define poetry as yet another art that pulls attention to the medium, language, defamiliarizing it from its usual invisible, directly communicative and expository functions, thereby discovering it afresh, activating and liberating it. But it is in usual, directly communicative and expository language that this explanation is offered, and so seems paltry, and even if one cuts to the chase and says, "You don't tell a dancer *that's not how you normally move,*" the defensiveness concedes the point. What was the point?

I'm thinking of that exercise where you imagine there were but one person in a group who points, who understands pointing as the act that might send the gaze of others in a direction he indicates with his outstretched arm and indicating finger. But with each demonstration, all the others keep their eyes on him, even and especially on his extremity which repeatedly extends and goes rigid and to which he seems to want to draw attention. For these others, it is a kind of dance to do. There is no casting from the body with any part of the body something as divorced and immaterial as someone else's attention. He introduces pointing again and again, but it doesn't take. He makes strange asides like, It's as though to indicate had never been a transitive verb. (Note to Rufus Wainwright: a "Me and My Arrow" duet with one of Harry Nilsson's sons.) It doesn't send.

So, you know, pointing is a construct. The child looking not past the pointer finger proves it. The self is a construct. Often I am permitted to return to a meadow. Poetry is a construct. When you say your poem it somehow isn't the person I know speaking.

No one writing a poem, achieving pleasure in discovery of intention and pattern and melody and association and parallels and syntactic and other tensions, is trying to be someone else. But once made, the poem so made registers as speech. And lyric speech is always, rather mysteriously, someone else's. Someone with givens, in a world. Theocritus may have been the first to find an exterior figure for this transformation, particularizing the givens of that speaker, and of the milieu for poems. These givens are representative pretenses of poetry still.

The last of the things I like that Allen Grossman says in his famous and pretentious *Summa Lyrica*, or maybe he's quoting someone, is that in the social realm of speech we face one another, asking and answering and remarking and informing, in exchange. But in the realm of speech a poem opens onto, we all face forward. We look on. We are positioned toward the speech differently than as we stood in the world a moment before, the world we came to the poem in. It is not meant for us exactly, this speech. It's in the locative case. Not a word of it, but the condition of the speech itself: it points us elsewhere if we listen. We listen in. The doings there are ongoing. What is that place? The one behind the construct of the idyll.

On Man Roulette

Permitting Shame, Error and Guilt, Myself the Single Source

Man Roulette is down right now. The cameras don't seem to be working. If the prospect of video chatting one-on-one with a man somewhere in the world, a man with whom you may build a small relationship or virtual transaction more or less premised on mutual attraction and sexual interest, appeals to you as it does to me, and you confront this functional blackout, the logical solution is in substitutive logic, a hacker's logic, exchanging other words for man in the url. They aren't synonyms, exactly, that you come to know to try: you come to know to try the offensive categorical generalities of pornography, even where your own identity is inscribed, delimited. It is a safe assumption that there are imitation sites, mirror sites if that's what they are called, though the most obvious, gayroulette, doesn't open anything. But a second choice, boyroulette, redirects to pinkroulette, which I would have considered only well after cockroulette, for example, I am embarrassed to say; but pinkroulette.com is quite active, with several channels ongoing (or cylinders spinning?)—sixty users in each, apparently—and very nearly identical to the interactive site I discovered for myself in the summer of 2010.

The modus operandi of Man Roulette is quickly appreciated and even mundane, but what it affords and requires of its user is phenomenal, and apprehended only gradually. There is an incoming video image in the image box at the top left of the screen: *him*, he in his deeply underway life dialing you in, staying on you for the moment at least, your station one of the many. Each successive occupant of the incoming image box is called "Partner." (Substitutive logic pervades the whole endeavor, really, and is part of roulette erotics.) The outgoing video image in the image box beneath that one, at the bottom left of the screen: "You," as you appear on camera, as you have chosen to position yourself on this day, relearning that the lean of your head to the left lists to the right rather in the mirror picture, lit as you wish under the overhead wall lamp. I show my face, my entire face, in my image box, which puts me in a minority of users, and since so few do, I wonder if it is unwise to do so, and why. Anonymity is below the mouth, one concludes. I am in a still smaller minority for entering the fray entirely clothed. I look likewise for other faces, other men who like to disrobe later.

To the right of the video stream is a large text field. What you type and submit appears to you attributed to You. What he replies and enters comes from Partner. There is, as it turns out, a lot to say while watching Partner look at you watching. He is, to begin with, in a room of some kind, particular, contingent, "real." With art and clocks and books and pillows and cigarettes and mail and daylight, or lamplight, with a bed or desk or basement sofa, with doors you can ask him to open, bags he may or may not empty, of content you may deduce about. The bottoms of his socks are dirty. You give it to him that his socks are dirty, that his door is ajar, that his grin is telling. "Partner: Are you for real?" The quite separate utility of the text field in Man Roulette returns credibility to the Cartesian mind/body divide, (even as opposing theories of self are likewise validated here: the self as instantiated only when relative to others in microcontexts, identity as entirely a matter of performance). Something for sure shifts into gear once the hunter-gatherer channel-surfing gives way to a single engagement and You and Partner partner up; a familiar compartmentalization may be experienced afresh: See something, say something.

The image boxes are a font of eidetic fantasy and comparative self-regard, a kind of fuel for the text field in which you create and remark and send, then watch for effect. The transcript of the date has its slow build here; reading it over later, if you cut and paste and save, you can recall his smile at certain points in the play, a particular surrender, a fidget, a sigh. You can recreate sensation. The text field is where the evening is spent, and the image boxes are where the night ends, typically. A sleepy last look, a wistful goodnight mouthed. If a date, it has been a date in which the two of you exchange as in confrontation but show simultaneously as adjacent, facing outward, as in a journey. The text field is the steering wheel, the handling, and the wending road at once; and your image and his are the chassis and heavy engine, the cruising velocity, the arrival. Partner and I filled evenings and long nights in the text field during the summer and fall of 2010. I know I fell in love on Man Roulette at least once, thought about Partner days on end, and I can recall real, breathing moments together in which I felt Partner fall for me: Albert in Detroit; Diego in Guayaquil, Ecuador; Sean in Franklin, Massachusetts; Bruno in Ouro Preto, Brazil; John Patrick in Milan. "Partner: you are not like other guys."

Man Roulette is down right now. Try other words for what you want, other words for what you are. Boy is a redirect, but it takes you there. It was on Man Roulette I learned I was an older man, an older man fantasy for some, a station to move right past for many others. Though I had had only younger lovers and boyfriends for some time, I think I hadn't realized I was no longer young myself that summer. On Man Roulette I was a mustache and a hesitation to smile. I was vain about my hair. The light was best at my desk upstairs. I swiveled into it at key moments. I said thirty-five instead of thirty-six, when asked. I swiveled. In the text field, I would race to establish an unexpected mix of permissive mischief, acute sensitivity and oblique non sequitur, to wager at intervals something true and peculiar about him or his situation. I was, in contrast to Partner, a good deal more controlling,

I came to realize, and much more invested in how I came across, and—however much I love to divulge to a stranger—less willing to risk. Partner I liked for being legible in his expressions, for his inability to contain himself, for his freedom in his rooms, for what seemed a freedom from tactics, for his relaxing inhibition.

Meeting someone on Man Roulette and maybe Skyping with each other for a few more dates is, in the end, for all its anonymity and performativity, no different than other love and sex relations, I find. I mean, people find their positions rather naturally vis-à-vis one another. I am, and was that summer, what my friend Maggie once termed a social passive top. (Which sounds like one of eight possible combinations, the most smug of the eight, although private active bottom sounds pretty self-involved too.) I think she meant, I'm scripted to be the catch; to draw in rather than pursue; and then, sure of his interest, to assert a kind of self-governance and skill at scaffolding, building a kind of domicile I can invite him into, a narrative usually, a construction of *us* with great focus on why he is special enough to belong, very pleasurable for both of us if Partner is dispositionally complementary. I'm attracted to his pleasure. I give him, in short, a fair amount of what I always want and routinely prevent, the experience of being fully seen and understood. You're lucky if you can read the script you're acting out.

What is different about Man Roulette is vantage, a kind of inherent third-person perspective on the both of you and your date. You get to see it all. An overburdened pair of blue briefs in Guayaquil, a candy wrapper with funny Italian. You have to oversee it all. His reaction reading your remark, your impulse to get a reaction. It took me a month and a half to tell my therapist what I had been doing. I said it was probably trivial, but we saw it was human.

On Withdrawal

Permitting Shame, Error and Guilt, Myself the Single Source

To withdraw—when it doesn't take an object, like: an offer, or a question, or the troops—to withdraw, as an intransitive verb, is, as it happens, always reflexive. If I withdraw, I withdraw myself. From what? From the race for city council, from active cocaine dependency, from the relationship, from the chill night air. To withdraw is to vacate what has held or kept you, and implies movement away from that engagement. Pullback.

When I can, on a commuter rail line, I sit in a rear-facing seat. I like the illusion of being drawn from the present into the future. To sit there is to withdraw. I have my eye on what I've left. There's that famous passage in Annie Dillard's *Pilgrim at Tinker Creek* when she's on the little footbridge over the rushing, swollen stream during the heavy spring snowmelt, when she asks what sort of idiot would rather look downstream from that bridge, at what's already passed beneath you rather than upstream toward what's coming. I think of this sometimes when I watch the scenery recede from a rear-facing seat, and feel a bit perverse for my predilection. Am I a withdrawn type, not as take-charge as Annie Dillard? By that comparison, almost certainly. But to so reason seems reductive, since, in effect, to choose to take the train to Natick, MA, from Back Bay Station Boston is the principal act of agency involved. The train is moving on its track no matter which direction you point yourself within it. To face forward is redundant if you are already forward-moving.

Dozens of times, during the academic year 2011–12, I took the MBTA line from Back Bay Station Boston to Natick, MA, riding with my back to my destination. I worked that year at

a fine arts boarding school: the first time, after nine consecutive years teaching at universities, that I had ever taught high
school. I directed the creative writing program, one of the five
arts programs at the school. Situated in a stern residential town,
the campus was formidably old and manicured, damp and dichro-
matic—as if the green of the lawns and the Puritan white of the
wood buildings had suppressed other color—and the students,
even the most spirited theater kids, were correspondingly more
than a little depressed, it seemed to me. My students, the writers,
were known as the most morose, the least social. Eating disorders
were alarmingly rampant and severe. It had been a girls' school, a
feeder for Wellesley College about a mile away, before converting
to coed and fine arts in the Eighties.

There were a lot of rules, and a complex, elaborate system of
retribution: penal councils, governance boards, response teams,
and levels of probation. All activity had to be documented, passes
and permissions obtained for liberties like a chaperoned outing
to the Natick Mall. All meals were in the dining hall at tables
for eight colleagues. One vegetarian option per meal. Two cis-
terns of soup. White crimini mushrooms ever in their bin at the
salad bar. The adults were a fair distribution, (though, curiously,
many shared the same name: Cathy or Ann) and all were quite
responsible—some more dynamic or more drab than others, some
detached and some officious—but not, on the whole, a faculty
you might imagine for an arts school. Perhaps we were too busy
or authorized with too much responsibility to parent and super-
vise to give free reign to our eccentricities. I don't know. I felt I
did not belong. I'm ashamed to say that I suspect my colleagues
thought rightly of me that, when I was scheduled for Sunday
morning work duty supervision or asked to present program suc-
cesses for alumni or donors or parents on Founders Day or Trustee
Weekend, my ego was bruised and my resentment enflamed, no
longer the college professor and acclaimed poet. Also, the work

was more stressful than any I had had, inexperienced as I was with being an emotional ballast for a group of teenagers and an administrator in profit-making education. Moreover, John and I were sure within months we'd made a mistake moving to Boston, which we found uptight and clenched and almost entirely joyless. I quit in early spring and told my students one day late May. We'd move to Tucson, where, unemployed for months on end before taking an office job, I have hidden my new fixation on building a narrative of a career not in decline.

I told them on a Friday, before the day-students left for the weekend, before the train took me back to Back Bay, and we discussed my decision around the Studio table, and through many tears, and even eventually expressions of gratitude or wistfulness, the girls shot one another glances that meant, "Now this!?" or "Are there no adults we can count on?" or "This abandonment compounds my general condition of abandonment." Maybe one "Can we go now?" All the writing students were female; I don't know why. As one of the primary men in their life, but openly gay, I was somewhat irrelevant to their developmental need to impress a male authority (or so said my therapist once); but perhaps they came therefore more quickly to the implicit understanding that I could be an arbiter and coach of their literary giftedness, if not of their success as practicing women. We grew compatible. They especially enjoyed *Pilgrim at Tinker Creek*. Remember the blubber-slathered knife Dillard recalls the Eskimo buried to the hilt to bleed the wolf dead? They liked that lick of inquiry.

One of the last days of school, after workshop, one of the girls was playing a popular Youtube clip of a marriage proposal on the large desktop in the rear of Studio 1. The proposal is in essence a live musical number, some six minutes long, a viral sensation, a meme maybe. The bride-to-be is seated on the tailgate of a truck that moves very slowly down a suburban street, her legs dangling. The camera is set up on the truckbed behind her at an overshoulder angle that captures some of her expression and most of the action that unfolds and follows the truck, as it enters the purview of the bride. Some musicians trail the young woman, walking at the truck's pace, in formation. Then, a color guard and drum corps fall in and march for a segment of the song that many voices sing, then fall away, leaving a soloist, who gives way to a couple of clowns juggling, or whoever has been choreographed next. An acrobat, an accordionist, close friends flown in whose sudden appearance in the number make the woman cover her mouth in wonder, both sets of parents I think, and other players prepared to enter the scene in flanks of backward walkers who perform and then peel off as someone else takes center stage advancing down the middle of the blacktop road. Everyone singing the girl's name in celebration. It is Bollywood in its excess, a marching version of "Oh Happy Day" crossed with a Rube Goldberg contraption and an episode of *This Is Your Life* on wheels. Finally, the groom, who has directed the performance, the feat of which is remarkable (you keep reminding yourself as his girlfriend is affianced), who had gotten everything right, occupies the screen alone with the fixed right shoulder and cheek of his beloved, as the truck comes slowly to a standstill. He gets down on one knee, on the asphalt, takes her hand, and asks the question more or less inaudibly. She cannot remove her other hand from her mouth at the end, shaking, nodding consent.

I watched, standing behind the four or five girls crowded in at the desktop, all of them grinning the smile of transfixion unsurpassed yet by scorn. Me too, I suppose. For the bride, advancement in time is backward-looking, and the surprise narrative is concerted effort unforeseen, falling in formation from the curbs which must have been lined a half mile with rehearsing players counting themselves in, reaching their marks, color coordinated with someone across the street. The parade leaves nothing behind, by design. It was all a dream.

I have to turn around, away from the computer, to position myself to think of the driver. What did he see out of his windshield as he kept his four-mile-per-hour pace? Did he watch the double yellow line? Did he look at his cellphone? Did he get out of the truck after parking it, careful not to close the door and jar the camera? Did he hear her yes? Did he pull forward across the finish line afterward, and drive home, or give anyone a ride? Was he best man material? Would *he* marry; could he? When he sees the playback, does he remember his own experience, pulling away from the show, driving between the players readied in the little lawns, all that rehearsal behind his careful haul? He is both the man staring downstream instead and the footbridge threshold itself. I like imagining him, while all the legs dangle out the back, in the fragrant warm day nature itself seems to them to have arranged.

On Tumbleweed

Permitting Shame, Error and Guilt, Myself the Single Source

Yesterday, a tumbleweed blew right up to my driver's side door, at a stoplight, here in Tucson. Simpson westbound, turning onto the highway frontage road north. I was alone at the light. Two hours prior, a hard decision, I turned down the offer of a three-year Visiting Poet position at a prominent creative writing MFA program a thousand miles away. I got out of the car, chased it a little ways in a subsequent gust, and then fit it into the backseat of my Mitsubishi, where it crumbled a bit in tight captivity. It was my lunch hour—I work a support position at an arts nonprofit downtown—and I brought it home with me. Later, my boyfriend John and I decided we would string it up as a chandelier in our living room. It's December 21st and we'd been wondering whether we'd get a tree. What does it mean when the universal symbol of itinerancy knocks into you the day you committed to stay awhile?

The flicker of the firelight will throw the tumbleweed's shadow complexly on the ceiling is my hunch, giving the room a little twirl and flutter. I'll suspend a tiny mirrored disco ball within it. One ornament spinning within another. I want to show it to John even more than I want to see it.

When I met John's father, Edmund, when he and his wife Diane, John's mom, visited their son in Montana about this time two years ago, his first words to me, over the handshake, were: "*So. Visiting. Poet?*" I felt it as a challenge, just as twenty minutes later, when dinner was over, he'd outwit me to pay the check. He knew I had been John's teacher, and I was uneasy in any misapprehension that our romance began when he was my student. I made sure to narrate the timeline as naturally as I could over our plates of river trout, and it was in that discernible anxiety I felt myself fall farther in Ed's early estimation. It seems to me that of all his children, John is most like him: unpredictable conversationally, apt equally to quip obliquely or to wander off on his own in thought—a peppery kind of depressive, stubborn, quick enough to be disappointed in the world, good enough to prompt others to show him any flair for transcending the ordinary. John is made that way, too, except in his demeanor he is more graceful, more liquid, lovelier. It is clear that Edmund loves John supremely. A *visiting poet*, might by definition leave new relations by moving on, this visiting poet who presumably had upswept his son in poetry or something, his son whom he had known all twenty-nine years theretofore and had been unable to save from every hurt or letdown.

Visiting Poet is a volatile term, term after term. At Purchase College in 2002 I had my first "visiting professor" position and was called Writer-in-Residence. As I recall, it paid $3,500, to teach a semester of poetry workshop. I rode the subway to the commuter rail at Grand Central to White Plains, where I caught a bus to Purchase to teach my two-hour weekly class. Then, at Pratt Institute of Art, I was Visiting Assistant Professor of Poetry, which was a designation beneath Adjunct and subject to more limiting union restrictions, although I was also advertised as Core Faculty. I taught two courses per semester and made around $14,000 per year and learned to collect unemployment in the summers, another six grand. I *visited* from a couple of neighborhoods away. For two of those three years, I lived in an SRO in Park Slope and still needed to supplement teaching income with freelance copy editing work. I moved to Los Angeles in 2006 and taught at both Cal Arts, where I was Visiting Faculty, and at Otis College of Art and Design, where I was Senior Lecturer, essentially an adjunct position, Core Faculty again. I averaged about $34,000 a year the two years I was in LA; it was the first time I had earned, in thousands, a salary greater than my age. (I had worked in publishing before teaching.) When I moved to Montana to be Richard Hugo Visiting Poet and then, subsequently, Visiting Assistant Professor of Poetry (again), I was working less than I had in some time, but was finally, officially, full-time, also often referred to as Replacement Faculty during those three years another poet was on leave. I made some proportion of her salary, the most in my career: $52,000. I rented a whole house, I had insurance, I got therapy. In the last two years, I have been the runner-up for tenure-track positions at two universities, Hobart and William Smith Colleges and Depaul University. When the first didn't come through, I took a high school program directorship, for $55,000, in Boston, which John and I endured only the one year (see Withdrawal). When I was passed over the second time, we moved to Tucson.

We live on the western edge of town, in a sparsely developed area without streetlights at the foot of the Tucson Mountains, at the immediate margins of the Saguaro National Park. On the other side of Gates Pass, over the closest mountain, down a winding road, is Old Tucson Studios, the most recognizable set of buildings in American cinema and television, and the most widely exported visual idea of American frontierism. Most anything with a wagon wheel or stagecoach or mercantile store or holster or headdress or petticoat was shot here. Certainly more formative impressions of tumbleweeds originated here than anywhere else.

When I was little, tolerating reruns of *Gunsmoke* or *Bonanza* on a sleepy Sunday after church with my grandparents in Virginia, or crushing excruciatingly on orphan Albert and his wet lips and eyes in *Little House on the Prairie*, on my own if I could arrange it, the tumbleweeds crossing the dusty main road were expressly incidental to the action, the epitome in fact of nature's indifference. As such, their desultory course through "town" could be used, directed, to lend whimsy or lonesomeness to the scene they were an integral part of setting. I assumed they were soft, fluffy, light enough to be carried on a breeze, like overgrown dust bunnies or dandelion heads maybe, but with more structural integrity. They rambled long distances, without disintegrating. On country radio in those early Eighties, Juice Newton sang to the tumbleweed, stretching *weed* into six syllables on the lilting melody. "You're living a cowboy's dream / freedom is the air you breathe…[but] you don't stop long enough / to let yourself fall in love." I live now among those incidental, airborne conclusions we all drew.

Tumbleweed is not a species, like ragweed or cinquefoil. There is, more likely, a tumbleweed genus, I'd imagine, a *family* of desert shrub that dries out in maturity and is eventually disunited at the narrow stem from its root system and rolls away in the first gust of many that motivates its final tour of earth, whereupon and only then it is known, in the singular form, as *a* tumbleweed. The tumbleweed is not soft, and not fluffy. This one, at least, has many barb-like thorns along its several long, fine, jointed limbs, and nearly as many crusted-over buds, long since flowered, though seeding may yet be a function of the tumbling afterlife of the bush gone polygon. As it rolls, the exoskeleton of the plant—which, in life, grew so intra-concerned because the tiny branches, by virtue of the stiff little thorns and offshoots, perverted the elongation of one another, bending ever inward—is further compressed and rounded by its overland travel. As an entity, however, the tumbleweed is not simplified during this reduction; this one has apparently ensnared and incorporated two or three stalks from similar plants it must have encountered. It is, while it rolls, entanglement amok.

When I started teaching at Pratt, it coincided with my breakup with Douglas, my longtime boyfriend in Brooklyn. When I left New York for Los Angeles, I left my ex-boyfriend Brett, as well; I left him my apartment, my stereo and records, my bed, my rug.

I wrote him letters from my new life. Both breakages were messy and incomplete, compounding the trauma of other separations I had made, wherein I had relied on my career—its demands and opportunities—to structurally necessitate or explain my absence or evacuation from someone or something, never offering the full account of self that would honor that relationship and my own needs, if indeed I understood them. To be in Montana meant separating and finally severing, after the protracted disenchantment of a long-distance partnership, from Doug in LA. I had thought then that commitment was what I needed to try; but, it was and has always been *honesty* about my own emotions that I owed to him, and others before him, and to my grandparents (who are weak, ill and dying now) and extended family to whom I have never revealed my adult self but have only moved farther away, to the city, to the west, into more remote territories of poetry and the academy, too incompletely realized to judge properly, too far to reject, too busy at Christmas to visit.

We have *this* one secured six feet above my head at the moment, suspended by its vestigial stem. The heat blowing from the highest air duct spins the tumbleweed counterclockwise, revolving the little mirror-plated orb within. John has just come in, after hours in his studio down the hall, to report that in a letter describing his own book project he "talked about time as a vessel for desire." We do a small dance, a joint endeavor, before I finish my paragraph, having held my thought, or mingling it with another. "You writing?" he asks.

On Containment

Permitting Shame, Error and Guilt, Myself the Single Source

A few things became clear in the moments and months after I was attacked by a dog at age nine. Within months, it was clear that my consequent fear of dogs had engaged a far greater fear. Within moments, it was clear that the dog, our dog, Sam, was my father's dog, loyal to him foremost. Sam, a mature, blue-black purebred Chow, rushed to the door one evening just as I did, to meet my father who had been away a while. My mother was in the kitchen. We had just moved back to Charlotte, from Paris, Tennessee, undoing the relocation we all had made when he left Roadway to work for Transcon nine months earlier. He was sort of *at large*, still, out on days-long interstate truck runs and still stationed in Tennessee, without us, orchestrating the sale of the life that never quite took. The tractor trailer he parked outside shook the Charlotte house a bit. At the back door, his dog and his son had both come to welcome him; and when he appeared there, Sam turned to his rival in the tight space of the mudroom and in a single motion, prefaced by a low growl, seized and ripped the flesh off the right side my face, cheek to jawbone—so that in the stunned minutes thereafter both of my parents would later say they could see my clenched back teeth when my mouth was closed.

Sam was banished instantly to the back lot, or retreated there ashamed, confused; and swiftly we made preparations to ride to the emergency room. Despite spilling blood and saliva where my face had been, I was numb to the pain, doing as I was instructed, completely mobile, cooperative with the towels, functioning in shock. On my father's lap—so rarely availed to me—in the passenger seat, as my mother drove, I was prevented from flipping the visor down to see the damage in the mirror but repeated often that one desire, to see for myself what was clearly disturbing my parents, neither of them even thirty years old, it now occurs to me, the year they divorced. *What was the damage* was the question, yes, but also, *What does it look like inside me?* I could hardly contain myself.

A plastic surgeon was airlifted in, and that night I had reconstructive surgery, and came away sewn up with many stitches inside and outside my mouth. A phenomenal operation, everyone said. It was 1982, and with insurance then, I suppose, a secretary and a truck driver could afford it. I was swollen and in bandages for weeks, a pathetic, dopey monster at school for a while; and then the wound became scar and for the next eight years tightened and traveled from my cheek to my chin as I grew into the face I have. There are a lot of nerve endings gathered in it, and it drives me a little crazy, distributes a sort of unsettling, illocable energy within, when a lover plays with that part of my face. I feel the same about my navel.

It's my recollection that the Winicottian psychologist and essayist Adam Phillips himself extrapolates broadly from his analysis of *tickling*; but, if not, the generality I have found so insightful is mine: beyond any fear is a greater circumambient fear—a terror—that one will be insufficiently able to hold that fear. That if the stimulus is present and ongoing, unchecked, one might fall apart, come to pieces, in her faculties disintegrate. In sustained tickling we know (we learned) there exists an outer lip or membrane between the simpler immediate excitement of fear and the shameful and complete loss of bodily control and mental composure. That sensible, pleasurable brim of containment is what makes tickling a good study for Winnicott's concept of *holding*, his determination that healthy child development needs a responsible, aware, caring adult "good enough" to hold (to stay with and make room for and validate and *check*) a child's pleasures and fears and emotions and acknowledge even the most confounding of them—in the child's independent trials and explorations—as in-bounds and worth expressing, and worth celebrating, in their human specificity. Without such a parent, if a parent has diminished capacity, or is narcissistic or in trauma or private crisis or absent altogether, protective self-sanctity is a greater necessity, sooner, and the child's retention of control, for instance, can be acute and maladaptive and difficult to reverse. On into my twenties I can remember struggling to destroy a kind of metaphysical conviction that disclosure was the enemy of integrity.

Proprioception, the term Charles Olson made famous for poetry, is the sense of the body's orientation and balance and the weighted proportion of its parts. Knowing I face forward is proprioceptive. Interoception is the sense one has of what is inside him. If I have pain in my urethra from dehydration, or if my heart skips a beat, it is interoceptive sensitivity that detects it. A friend of mine who recently confided to me that he has tested HIV positive described how he *knew* the flu symptoms he had in November were more than flu. He knew something was different inside. He said he even knew the moment, weeks after contracting the virus, he seroconverted. He described this interoceptive sense as body-consciousness, but couldn't say where he felt it. He didn't need to, to make himself understood. Likewise, where is fear, or desire, or grief, if not inside? *I know it is within, because I contain it.* My enabling delusion as a child, essentially, was that affective experience was like a pain in the gut or a lump in the throat: it was something inside yourself that you could choose to hold in.

In Charlotte we shared the neighborhood with a number of large, ferocious dogs. This was true before the bite and I was wary of them then; but, afterward, in my presence, it was as though they were lit up with bloodlust and rage. In particular there were a pair of German Shepherds and a Doberman Pinscher along my walk to the bus stop, and each morning seemed to be the morning that one would finally vault the fencing that barely kept him in. Naturally, I was terrified of what could happen if any of them got to me, and their threat was utterly convincing. Walking in a group was worse because, sauntering apace with everyone and even keeping up conversation as we passed, I nonetheless set off the savagery of the animals around us, and it could not be denied. It could not be covered with my pretenses to normalcy. When they charged, it was obvious they were charging me; it was evident their nasty, murderous mania had an object and I was it. Even today, I feel the need to point out that my performance was flawless. I know I betrayed no trepidation in my mien or manner. I was very good and well practiced at keeping it in. When an older boy said it aloud, and when I worked out what he meant, I felt my situation grow in dimension: *He smells your fear.*

Early on you have a secret. It is almost as though the secret is there before you. You are ever in relation to it; you are its container, and because by definition the one imperative is that you cannot share the secret—perhaps you develop the understanding that no one in your small world may be entrusted with the knowledge of what's inside you—you become, through and through, a holding environment for the secret. It is so intrinsic that you could not, at so young an age, begin to know how to explore it. How you feel is the secret. Or, it is not untrue to say, the secret is how you feel. Because when someone asks how you are feeling and you cannot say, you can see them try to access what's inside; and it troubles you enough to close tighter, or cover more. Your little mastery over it you know to be a life-or-death matter. It is the end, the very edge of abyss over which you send yourself, if the contents are accessed. Then, one day, you wake up to the new reality that walking the same Earth you have lived on all these years, growing increasingly proficient as the keeper of your contents, is at least one creature endowed with the singular ability to sense something you are concealing for your life, a creature whose report is loud as a gun. It smells your fear.

In its presence I could not contain myself. Even then, starting then, with new dread, I felt myself; I couldn't have said by what extroversion, but I knew eventually I was coming out.

What was that going to look like?

At the end of *King Lear*, a mirror is brought to the face of good Cordelia, to be consulted. Lear calls for it, disbelieving the worst. At the beginning of the play, when she tells him that she cannot be *wholly* devoted to him—that she will need to divide her devotions, in loving her self and her eventual mate, as well as her father the king—he replies that honesty alone will be her dowry then. Honesty is what she is left with, disinherited. A birthright for one entitled to nothing. At his own tragic end, after Cordelia is presented to Lear, with the news of her death, the looking-glass is brought, on his command, to her face—closer: to her mouth. There is a moment, a last viable moment, before the *glass* is withdrawn, having captured no vapor from what would have been her breath, that the mirror is called a *stone*. A repurposing happens. The mirror is not a depth *into* which to view the reflection of one's composed façade, but, rather a surface *on* which to manifest what comes from within.

There is only the one conclusive turn in the mortal story, I suppose. Before that one, because of that one, there are a number of opportunities, precisely when one is petrified, to break the glass.

On House Sitting

Permitting Shame, Error and Guilt, Myself the Single Source

In the early spring of 2002, when I housesat for my friend Rodney, I arrived at his studio apartment in Provincetown just after Eileen Myles had left, apparently. I found and would later return the keys where she had left them, by house rules, on a hook under the sandy back stairs. I hadn't yet become friends with Eileen, but I learned from her that week that a nice thing to do is to leave a little gift with a poem or a note for the permanent resident to find on his return. Beside Eileen's envelope, I too left Rodney some ephemeron or other I had found, a scrap of map or something, as well as a poem I set my sights on writing that icy week, a poem set there where "back street runs along front street, flaring." I found a book I liked on the narrow shelf of art books in the apartment, called *The Boston School*, a monograph on a group of contemporaries a generation older than me: Jack Pierson, Nan Goldin, David Armstrong, and the artist I saw in a show with David Wojnarowicz once, who died like him of AIDS. The book gave onto an underworld of elective affinities, image after image in a denuding share of splendid light, the fabric of the mattress ticking fraying against the floor, junk in the blood. Where were they all; some place—not *Boston*—united them, a *scene*, a life. A concluding essay by Eileen herself was effortlessly brilliant. That thin, heavy paperback fed me; I jerked off imagining myself into situations in the Armstrong photographs, on Rodney's bed, or more likely at the little desk at the window; and I carried it with me on walks to the diner and the fireside bear bar—showing myself hiding behind it—and read it in my knit gloves under the flagpole at the town square. Maybe there was a plant to water, or mail to set aside; but I don't think so. Still, to be there when Rodney couldn't be was vaguely understood to be as much favor to him as to me. I had housesat his Seventeenth Street place in the city, too; I could care like family for his things. Eileen at Rodney's, then myself.

Commensalism, or mutual benefit, is a constitutive premise of housesitting, or maybe an enabling fiction. The housesitter is apt to recognize the opportunity as a private windfall, and the pleasure is tandem: first in his own dis-habituation, and then in the adoption of a new readymade home, a vacated life to try on. With the extra keys on his chain, the housesitter leaves work on a different train or by a new road, becomes a local in the café or dogpark, creates—or stars in—fantasies grown out of his new neighbors' notice. In the new routines, a film has been removed from his self-understanding; he is available to experience. Initially, everything about housesitting is *citational*, as though in each activity in the house one carries quotation marks above his shoulder blades, like campy angel wings. Here I am "drawing the blinds," now I think I'll "separate" these "twist ties"; who am I exactly "taking" a "bath"? There's a Japanese word, auxiliary verb I think, that Tom Spanbauer introduces in a novel, I can't remember which, and I can only vaguely recall the babyish sound of the word; I think it translates loosely to "play at," and is used to signal a sense of low-stakes doing: I'm playing at making toast. (It's not really going to be good, and I'm not toasting it seriously.) It's perhaps akin to the American millennial "all" or "all like": *She was all like, "keep your eyes on your own page."* (Her perturbed manner was unsuited to my abiding penchant for detachment.)

In housesitting, you have an established normalcy to play at, an established normalcy to play against. Largesse and obligation alternate and conspire in your transitory identity, which wanders the premises with you: minder, keeper, prowler, visitor, charlatan, surrogate, subordinate, beneficiary, help. Because, as you move through the days, the eventual goal is to cover all traces of yourself and leave things as they were, house sitting is situationally criminal, or adolescent at best, surreptitious in any case. The construct is a tidy, socioeconomic parallel of queer desire in the twentieth and twenty-first centuries.

I've lost at least one friendship, albeit not a long or close one, because of unmet housesitting expectations. An older student, Lyn, in a poetry master class I taught several years ago, had generously offered me use of her Tucson home so that I could in effect extend my arts residency a week longer. She and her husband lived in the foothills but had this beautiful second home near the university, with lots of large vivid art on the walls, hardwood floors, air-conditioning, wi-fi, a modern kitchen, and a nice side patio. When her husband let himself in in the middle of the day, a day before Lyn signaled they would return—I stirred out of their bed, sotto voce telling Jeremy to stay put, dressing myself hurriedly—he was already assessing the state of things in his house: a rug had been rolled up (for more yoga and dance space), a dining table had been appropriated as a desk, the stereo was looping an unfamiliar playlist, outside the patio chairs were helter-skelter and a dish was refashioned as an ashtray, and the leavings of breakfast were everywhere. Lyn's husband and I had never met, and we startled one another; and as I explained barefoot that I was given the clear impression that my stay was meant to last another day, and requested time to pack and properly tidy and replenish the groceries I had used, and (gesturing behind me) to finish visiting with a friend, he was very put out and said the misunderstanding was mine and asserted his plans to return in an hour, dialing his wife at once, audibly irate by the time he reached the driveway. I remember feeling reprimanded when Lyn told me later she was deeply disappointed. I had the uneasy sense that the apology elicited and that I gave was for sleeping with a man in their bed. In fact, Jeremy *had been* a lover of mine, from a trip to Tucson for a wedding a year earlier; and the stay that Lyn had helped me extend a week was spent helping him through the disgrace and confusion he felt reckoning with a very new, days-old diagnosis as HIV positive. I was the first person he had told, breaking down as he was removing our clothes the night we reunited. I held him all that night, through a terrible sleep, washed his tower of dishes in the morning, and promised to stay a while, until he was set up with help at the local Ryan White Fund center and had learned a bit about his options from his new counselor. It was an education for me too, and helped me confront a deep, formative fear. We fell into the habit of napping together, just being affectionate and warm, after a joint. I retrieved him from beyond the security gate at Lyn's in the afternoons. By day I wrote a poem, for him, which I printed at the Kinko's and delivered to Jeremy's porch before leaving town. I remember I exited the poem by "stepping out of the halo down around my ankles."

I think you could tell a rather comprehensive queer literary history through the lens of housesitting. Hart Crane on Columbia Heights wrote most of "Voyages" in his borrowed rooms, in the building belonging to the father of Emil Opffer, his beloved who would come and go, the building formerly occupied by the architect of the Brooklyn Bridge, and then, later, out on Long Island, cranking Ravel's *Bolero* on his Victrola and experimenting with enemas, until his friends the Gorham Munsons or the Malcolm Cowleys prohibited his return. Jack Spicer wrote off, two by two, his friends who left Berkeley for the suburbs to start families, rejecting, inveighing against their offers to relax for a stay in their homes when they traveled. "My tongue is sharpened on the iron edge. / Canaries need no trees. They have their cage." James Schuyler might have been committed or might have starved had his artist friends not offered their homes, again on Long Island, eventually establishing the Fund, which consolidated monies to keep him finally in his *own* apartment in the Chelsea, to pay his rent and the wages of an assistant who made D'Agostino's runs for him and made sure he had his meds and smokes and other basics. That assistant was Eileen Myles, and that daily care in 1979–80 was doubly important for poetry and queer literature. Thirty years later, Eileen detailed in the "career narrative" part of her novel *Inferno* a rather infamous housesitting stint, when her patrons felt she was not sufficiently grateful for the opportunity to caretake their Pennsylvania country home, however much she filled the frontmatter of her subsequent books with acknowledgment of the gift—for her, the gift of access was to the natural world, which she includes like Schuyler in her poem—poem as score of poet's doing, in candid flat field notation. "I always put my pussy / in the middle of trees." It's my guess the couple didn't really understand Eileen's aesthetic and ethos; maybe they took insult from it.

There is apt to be, in the mix of other feelings, *resentment* if either party involved is insensitive to what it might mean to borrow the stance and posture of cultural privilege, when a queer person or couple housesits for a straight couple or a heteronormative household. I remember my boyfriend at the time, Douglas, and I visited our queer friend Anna Grace, who was staying in Poughkeepsie in the home of poet Eamon Grennan and his wife, a classicist, both of whom taught at Vassar. Their address—One Wing Road—was already a poem, or a too droll joke it seemed to me, where everything about the place seemed so complete and tranquil. Their sunroom doubled as a remarkable library, every chair a reading chair, and each step through the house a wide plank creak of communication: a *family* is home. One day the cat got out, and with our help Anna worked up the courage to call Ireland and explain, as their daughter wailed in the background, that we'd found the feline corpse on the road. Hottest day of the year, and she'd been dead for hours. They instructed Anna where to bury her, under a favorite shrub, and with which toys; I made the cardboard coffin and worked up something to say graveside;

and that night as summer's odors wafted through the windows we worried we'd have to disinter and dig deeper, and redo the ceremony perhaps we hadn't taken seriously enough. Same thing happened visiting my friend Jason housesitting for his teacher Alison Deming. The cat had licked a puddle of antifreeze. It was awful.

Another time I visited Jason in the James Merrill House, now established by some kind of trust as a gay poets' residency, in coastal Connecticut. Merrill's last doctor's appointment was still scrawled on the kitchen whiteboard. He had moved to Tucson, a brief, final home.

Housesitting, like playing house, is identity rehearsal—practice, of course. For what? You're writing a future into a present, you're writing an other there onto the self here, and quote yourself back to yourself. Maybe there's a little prophesy in it. Years after my Provincetown encounter with *The Boston School* I began dating a photographer, Brett, whose day job was as David Armstrong's assistant, light meter reading and preparing the shoot at David's as one after another waifish, long-lashed, wounded-seeming, bothered, sleepless boy all neck and lip, rib and nipple, posed languidly in that wash of light I never would have thought streamed through Bedford-Stuyvesant Brooklyn. David trusted us with the keys to the brownstone all summer one summer. We called, *Where are you*, to each other across all four floors. We played like models, answering upstairs, "listening to the ice cream truck," in the bedroom "toweling off." Like David, Brett also makes portraits, mostly of young men on the margins, that attain a fictive dimension: I'm looking now at one on my wall in Tucson, taken in his Park Slope SRO apartment that once was mine, of a small-framed young man, probably a lover of Brett's, twenty maybe, with moist, accepting eyes wide on his simple face, his collar open to the divot top of the sternum, and falling behind him behind his black hair and left shoulder is a tendril of my old spider plant, slender-jointed and green. Brett's portraits, like David's, belong together, appreciably (they share a life, a scene—you gather these people all know and love another—though, we don't). It's not a word David would have used for the franchise of subjects united by *his* characteristic look, but I remember Brett calls us a *family*.

The poems in my second book, *A Several World*, the book I wrote in my thirties, default to first person plural; repeatedly I find I work myself into a we, and the we I mean is not usually "John and me"—us domestic life partners—but more like this queer kind of family that might connect Brett's photo subjects. Imagine an us conjoined in our respective appeal to this lover, this looker for signs he is not alone and need not be. It reminds me of medieval thought, when likeness (in appearance, in disposition, in leanings) was understood to be the effect of some kind of contact, metonymic not metaphoric in relation, something that passes via touch in a realm subtending this one, a contagion. A family attuned alike, who find each other eventually and dovetail their several courses far from families of origin: the we I mean in my poems, connected preternaturally, manifested similarly, recognizable to one another, is active in our trade of relations and interdependences, a guild, or troupe or battalion of us thrown together by like circumstances, managing perforce a solidarity. The young help the old, and the old help the young, likewise the vagrant and the situated, passing keys, leaving notes. "Here we are all by day. By night we're hurl'd / by dreams each one..." "Into a several world" Robert Herrick gave us bed as a place to be distinct; Whitman cited that same nightly tendency to separate as what we most share.

Welcome back, Rodney, Eamon, Eileen, Lyn, Alison, Brett. Jimmy, David, Jeremy, welcome home.

On Minutes

Permitting Shame, Error and Guilt, Myself the Single Source

Minutes are so called because they keep chronological record, or because they guarantee that the proceedings of a meeting will be represented in their minutiae. They constitute the primary mode of clerical documentary nonfiction narrative, and are understood to be entirely faithful to fact, objective and without analysis, very nearly at 1:1 scale. Nonetheless the art of preparing minutes inheres in one's facility with abstraction, namely paraphrase. There are no quotation marks in minutes. What was *said* must be *related*, and the audience is posterity.

Conversion from verbatim discussion or transcript to minutes involves most saliently the selection of choice predicates in dialogue tags. Mr. Gallin conceded, Mr. Cowen established, Ms. Faigen refuted, Dr. Ghory added, Mr. Glaser reasoned, Ms. Birger replied, Mr. Kasser continued, Mr. Wrentmore determined, Ms. Flatt commended. An executive, nonliterary restraint attends the entire practice: "demurred" or "intoned" or "capitulated" or "deflected" would be too dramatic, attuned to the quality of the remark in its scenic context, not to the quality of its function in the business at hand; nor is it proper to note when a participant "gasped" or "stammered" in her conversation, and certainly not when he "smoothed back his graying, feathery hair along his temples, regaining composure." "Listened" is not a verb for minutes. There *are* verbs in minutes outside of speech tags; but these are reserved for the performative speech acts of the meeting, sometimes known as action items, customarily set in bold type. The first action item occurs early in the minutes, when participants move to approve the minutes of the prior meeting. So moved.

Seconded. The minutes from the May 23, 2013, meeting were unanimously approved.

Before they are submitted for approval, minutes are said to be *kept* or *taken*, in the same way notes are; but minutes are also *prepared*, commonly, a term that is proper to reports, as well. Minutes are drafted but are not the work of a writer. They are the province of the secretary.

In November 2013, I deleted the words *Paris Review* and *The Nation* and *Harper's Magazine* from my résumé, and added PowerPoint and Excel, to better my chances for the full-time support positions I applied for in Tucson. For one, as executive assistant at a statewide performing arts nonprofit organization with a seven-million-dollar budget, I drove to the company's Phoenix offices to interview, and even though it was clear the position absorbed duties more proper to personal assistant and would mean aiding someone who was clearly attached to structures of subordination, Paul called the next day to offer me one thousand dollars more than I said I expected: $37,000. John and I had begun living on his social work salary alone and, after a four-month job search, it was necessary to take the first position I was offered. Seven months later, long after I regretted saying yes—indeed, the context was our preparation for a board meeting I would not attend, beyond the effective date of my resignation—Paul told me I had been the only person he interviewed who wasn't doused in perfume and who wasn't evidently just some bimbo. *Mr. Cowen commended the professionalism and discretion Mr. Blanchfield brought to the position, and remarked his facility with language and finesse in trustee relations.* "Bimbo," yes, off record.

Playing back the audio in fifteen-second increments, reconstructing in my document window a recent board meeting in short attributive prose paragraphs mostly devoid of the tension that would have actually suffused the management and staff and trustee interactions, attuned in the playback to Paul's nervousness at the table—which was apt to recklessly divert the room's attention to any associate he might call on for cover—sometimes I recalled my mother under her own headset in the secretarial pool at Smith, Helms, Mulliss, and Moore in 1983 Charlotte, one foot on the pedal that likewise advanced or paused the dictation in her ear. The voice would have been his who frequently ridiculed her lack of sophistication and once patted her blond head, good girl. After my parents divorced, she would take me to the firm on Saturdays when she could earn overtime and catch up on her workload with her boss present in voice alone. While she plugged into and worked her giant instrument, I too hovered over the ready hum of an electronic typewriter at a colleague's station she or another secretary prepared for me. It was heaven to feed the paper in, and begin conceiving my day-long story, always some derivative fantasy whose trademark stroke of original appeal was the inclusion as characters whichever of the firm's employees also showed on Saturday. In the morning, I would tour the floor and say hello to every one, including the attorneys, gathering impressions that I would transmute into the machinations of the wizards and damsels and squires and villains in my story. As I neared its conclusion, it was a thrill to anticipate the reactions of the office's professionals who would break in the afternoon to read the several sheets that I had photocopied, stapled, and distributed to my readership. I was courier of my own weird news. In each edition, the women (Barbara or Joan or Nancy or Sandra) by their own ingenuity and with the assistance of an unlikely male hero were freed from some peril or oppression. After a few minutes each reader would emerge from his office or her cubicle and gather around my mother's desk, to read passages aloud to each other, laughing or pantomiming the action. The writer at nine and his mother beamed. Debut publication.

A couple of the lawyers who came by the dozen to the Charlotte funeral home this May to pay their respects to my stepfather Frank told me at my penultimate position in the visitation line that they remembered well the Saturday stories some thirty years ago, last we had seen each other. I recognized Mr. Askew and Mr. Bowman. They asked about my life and career, and offered condolences for my loss. I thanked them on my mother's behalf, too, for coming, before they reached out to my right for her hands, visited with the woman who had been their pretty employee so long before, and then stood themselves at the open casket.

By that evening in the week, day three of my bereavement leave, fifteen hours before the funeral, I had managed to track time by the writing assignments that death brought me. With a couple of Frank's colleagues, I had synopsized in an obituary for *The Charlotte Observer* Frank's estimable career and many achievements in the Justice Department and in corporate tax law practice and on the board of the Arts and Science Council of Charlotte. And, earlier in the day in Frank's office, I revised the eulogy I had been writing and read it for my mother who had crept downstairs for a preview. I choked over the wording that spoke most to her experience of Frank. When I looked up from the document window, we were having our first genuinely connected interaction in more than fifteen years. Like something otherwise valueless I might have made as a child, she called it precious. Back in the visitation line that long evening, while I worked up something to offer back to each face facing mine, not ten feet from the corpse of my adoptive father of twenty-seven years, a consistent buzzing in my pants pocket was alerting me—I realized later, undressing for a third night in the bed where Frank last lay alive—to phonecalls and texts from a coworker asking at Paul's behest where in my office the tape recorder was. A joint executive and finance committee meeting had been about to begin in Arizona, where it was still afternoon.

"Paraphrase" is a lyric poem by Hart Crane that gets the sudden, lights-out fact of death right. Still, stultified, final, inborn. I read it again this summer. Reckoning like a Dickinson, it fabricates from the first stanza a tick-tocking in systole and diastole in the nameless subject whom the poet puts to bed and who never rouses. What "shall sometime flood / the pillow," in a horrible mislead, is shown by Crane to be morning light, which keeps coming, even as the poem ends observing the figure's white head as a "paraphrase" among the roses on the wallpaper it lies against, as lifeless as they. The word choice is inexplicable, querulous, oblique, just right. A paraphrase among the rows of roses—a relief receding there—renders their locked pattern a kind of language, but what can it say?; and the head in the place where the living being lay is nominated as this titular hermeneutic tool, useless as such without its objective genitive *of*. It cannot be said what original locution this paraphrase summarizes. A case, I think, for Crane, of Flesh Made Word again. A reversion. Revelation withdrawn.

"Dear Grace and Grandma" begin many of Crane's letters back to Cleveland, particularly those he wrote from the desk of his temporary day job as a typist producing something called *Sweet's Architectural Catalogue*, somewhere in Manhattan, the year he wrote "Paraphrase" and many of the other poems in *White Buildings*. 1923? Hart Crane's psychology was peculiarly inscribed by his life's circumstances: forbidden any more of his confectioner father's support, he worked nonetheless for Sweet's; and, as is often noted in conjunction with his death by drowning ten years later, he had been son of the inventor of the Life Saver, his last words that morning linguistically imparted a loss of his mother too: "I have been *disgraced*." I cringe a little for Crane in his letters home. He described to his mother and hers his frustration when his writer friends asked him how the writing was coming: they did not need to earn their income as office workers. They were a young man's letters, restless, posturing, championing encouragingly his mother's new life after the end of her marriage, recounting a compliment he received at a literary party, and then wishing for a job working on a ship like his lover Emil, away eight months at a time. He reported to them that when Emil next docked in New York Harbor, he would be returning to the news that his father had died, which would come as a considerable shock. Was it Mr. Opffer whose last night he imagined in para-phrase, whose son in sex he'd found eternity in?

Who tells the minutes? By custom, their point of view is third person limited, and their tense is simple past. The secretary refers even to himself in third person, by title and surname. No one recording proceedings was ever outside proceedings, binder after annual binder, for all posterity. Mr. Blanchfield is survived by his wife Sandra, 61, of Charlotte, and one son, Brian, 39, of Tucson, Arizona.

On Authorship

Permitting Shame, Error and Guilt, Myself the Single Source

One month after he died, I buried a brush that belonged to my stepfather. It was in the truck that I later drove four days and nights back to Arizona. The brush had always been in the truck, on the vinyl seat. One of those twirly wooden brushes, with bristles emitting radially all around the head. A man's brush, with many black and, later—only recently—gray hairs in it. To hold it in use is to grip it in one's fist, like a microphone. Or, perhaps there's another way. Brushing his hair was the final touch for Frank, who would make the six or seven coarse strokes over his damp head at thirty-five miles an hour, no mirror, on the way somewhere, the office, and toss the brush back onto the seat. I didn't like it to touch me.

My mother and I had been cleaning out the cab of the truck, before I was to take it to the car wash. Both doors wide open as we worked opposite each other. I asked what she wanted to do with the brush, and she said to throw it away along with a handful of empty wrappers to his lens cleaning pads and plastic caps to his Quik Stik insulin syringes. Instead, returning from the garbage bins at the side of the driveway, I squatted briefly and hid it by a pine tree and later, when she was gone on an errand, came out to get started.

The early summer ground in Charlotte is pretty soft and so it was easy by that pine tree, near the fountain Frank would have heard in quiet moments the last few years, alone only for the duration of an errand. What do others do in their unguarded moments? I worked a stick, a broken branch, into the ground, twisting it deeper like a rudimentary drill, about seven or eight inches deep. Then, pressed with the stick in circle motions against the well walls of the hole it had created, dilating it sufficiently to admit the brush, which I pushed in, handle first. As the bristles gave resistance, I stood and stepped on the top of the brush, and then the earth accepted the whole thing rather easily, snugly. Only the brown wood button top of the brush was at last visible. To bury it entirely seemed wrong somehow. Uncovered, it has a touch of authorship, this penny-sized honey-brown button above grade; and perhaps the organic, even potentially nutritive essence of Frank's hair is aerated a bit this way. It wouldn't push deeper in without special effort that would have been beyond pressing. I'll admit it was odd. But I like knowing about it there, this locally iconic instrument of his infrequent flair.

On the Leave

Permitting Shame, Error and Guilt, Myself the Single Source

The leave is a term in certain sports and games that proceed by turns or trades of agency—bowling, billiards, croquet maybe—a term which functions to connect any discrete play to the play before and thereby to the narrative of the contest. It is a narreme, like *denouement*. After any single shot, the leave, in billiards, is the arrangement of however many of fifteen numbered balls remain on the table, relative to the position of the cue ball, with respect to the planning for and execution of the subsequent shot. The leave is accounted qualitatively, assessed in terms of relative advantage and disadvantage to the player preparing to shoot. Good leave, lucky leave, bad leave, tricky leave, sorry leave, snookered.

The leave, of course, is what's *left*. In derivation it must have been backformed as a participial noun, but notably (like the *take* in a heist, the *getaway*) it retains an ongoingness; indeed, it applies to the game's continuation, it elicits. Effectively the leave is *the given* for him who must next address the cue.

In pool (*billiards* is for the yellow pages), if your shot has been successful, after the unpocketed balls have stopped rolling, the leave is what you have left yourself. If your shot has been unsuccessful you give your turn over to your opponent, and the circumstances are his to contend with. A mystery is embedded here. *Whose shot it is* is idiomatic to the game, never beyond determination; but, whose leave it is, per se, is not expressible. Something else it shares with "the given": the leave is repellent of pronouns. It belongs to the game. Where is it one first heard of the leave?

My father, Curtis, shoots pool, shot pool all through my childhood. He put a table in our house's spare room, converting it from the room where my mother had kept her Singer machine and dress forms, a room imaginable as a nursery, I suppose. It was too small for the table, really, and you often had to shoot down at the cue ball with your shooting elbow cocked high. I played with him a few times, but I could never hold my stick steady with any confidence, could never make a sufficient bridge with my left hand; I resorted to forming an OK sign with my forefinger and thumb, for the stick to glide through, the way children panto-mime "doing it" in the earliest notions of penetrative sex. This method required more baby powder than the dusting that was customary to keep the hands dry, and the scent made me feel even more disqualifyingly young, dewy. Perhaps on occasion he had friends over, but mostly my father played by himself, nine ball. I would revolve the table with him (his gravitational opposite), as the shots demanded, aware of opportunities to pass him the little blue cube of chalk; and then collect the balls from the six pockets when the game was done. With practice, I improved at racking the balls tightly for the next break. He frequently would run the table, which meant that he shot with strategic forethought and had superb touch when it came to the leave.

He was good enough to supplement his trucking income moonlighting as a resident pool shark at The Waterin' Hole on Tyvola Boulevard in Charlotte, during the late Seventies and Eighties. It is my memory that he was at The Waterin' Hole more evenings than he was at home with my mother and me; but, it wasn't until my parents' separation and divorce when I was nine or ten that I ever visited the place with him, during one of his custody weekends. It was daytime, memorably—whenever any-one entered the dim, windowless bar, the doorway shone like a nova, a fireball from which materialized one after another scrag-gly, mustached, leather-jacketed man with some time to kill. They were each like him, casually prepossessing, some younger and rougher-edged; it was a revelation to find that my father was family there. The bartender's name was Mama, in fact, and she called him Curt, as his own mother and brothers did and do. I saw it all with new eyes. It was night before I noticed the bar had filled (a sudden, quickening feeling I came later in adulthood to love); and as Mama served me a Sprite with a maraschino cherry, my father, no longer running the table, set me up on a stool and instructed me on guessing the ages of the prettier women who came up to the bar, guessing some number of years younger than my actual estimate, when he signaled. I was pleased to be clever (or at least good at subtraction), glad to be included in my father's home life, its component conspiracies. To be my father's son was to be his accomplice or else his unnecessary freight.

There were to be about two more years of partial custody. From age twelve on, I rarely saw my father, once every two or three years maybe, for an hour, at my grandmother's house. As the given condition of my young adolescence, I could deal with the relative privacy and self-dependence that afforded me, particularly around my flummoxing deficit of masculinity and my paralyzing and thrilling attraction to other boys. Understanding this given as the leave, it took me years to know how to play my turn.

By the time I was in college my father had become a good story, an unlikely one to those who knew me from literature class or from the critical theory quarterly; and I told it to maximize its absurdity. That my father had been a truck driver, a Harley rider, a grifter, a cad; that when he divorced my mother he got a perm, bought a Camaro Z-28, and moved into a singles apartment complex with HBO and a sauna; that he then dated much younger women—one woman in sailor blue and bodice lacing named Deanna had a daughter named Leanna whom she dressed identically; that twice later I learned he had remarried, to a twenty year-old and a nineteen-year-old—it could startle my peer group, which was eager to identify on the fringe. By the time I was in New York, and out, in my early and mid-twenties (well on into my thirties, really), I recognized that the story of my father could also twist or deepen someone's understanding of me, even elicit a kind of empathy; and the darker elements of the story, told candidly and modestly as if without judgment, could impress whomever I was getting to know in the bar. That the women my father dated were all notably damaged and of little means and more desperately heedful of his mood and attentions than I; that one moved in to his apartment with her young son, Mikey, whom I fantasized about protecting from the volatile storm of abuse that accompanied her there; that Mikey's father, in a sexually violent rage, had bitten off one of her nipples—which I should never have been told and have never forgotten; that my father and she would have distressingly loud sex in the next room while Mikey and I pretended to watch tennis on TV; that Jimmy Connors still reminds me of hatching a plan to run away with Mikey the next time we were to be dropped off at the vaguely criminal Putt-Putt course for the day; that soon after, he simply vanished and (the only betrayal I can remember feeling) raised no objection when contacted about my stepfather's petition to adopt a year later. Curtis's signature on the form to change my name looked effortless. I might include the detail about his dogs, each of whom, in succession, he had named Romeo. Some died, I guess, and some were sacrificed to breakups. The story, if I told it, began at the pool table, or from the bar overlooking it. *My father was a pool shark.*

I must have offered some of this at Excelsior and later across the street at Ginger's the night I remember most feeling like (and most relishing feeling like) *trade,* like a new man emerging from the magma-bright doorway at The Waterin' Hole, adjusting his eyes to the dark inside and its notice of him. My friend Eliot had just started dating this guy, who brought along his friend from Manhattan to our neighborhood bar. It was soon clear that he and I were disinclined to like each other and were intermixing for our friends' sakes only. He said he was a high-end residential real estate agent, parkview penthouses chiefly, and made a conscious, fussy show of slumming it in Brooklyn that night, laughed when I offered to buy a round. He was surprised that anyone read poetry anymore, and was unrelentingly incredulous that I should be a professor, an intellectual, if that's what I was, looking me over. He too liked to be teased and enjoyed performing his scandalized horror if I shared something rather *low* or, as the evening wore on, dared to turn from aloofness to point-blank directness, full frontal. I was a strong swiveler. He was quick and queeny and slight and superior and I wanted him to want me. It was against the pool table near last call that he pressed into me; apparently he could be scandalized equally by his own behavior, a uniquely queer attribute I love. It's the act of his open mouth and widening eyes I most remember about his reaching down into the top of my jeans. Four hours of circling one another and fifteen minutes of kissing had aroused me several times to the point of pre-cum. I was lodged in the band of my underwear and slick with it. He jerked me off then and there and made sure the three or four others in the room could see.

Affirming a kind of brotherhood we have, my friend Matthew recently helped me reel in the this anecdote's true conclusion: It is a particular sensation of sluttiness to head home in jizzy jeans.

This would have been early winter 2005. I was the same age Curtis had been when he'd sat me up on the barstool and learned the sexual edge he had thereby. Albeit more indirectly, *his* part in *my* profile had likewise become mine to exploit. I played what I had. I could motion to him if to be wanted wanted him. Stripes and solids are six ounces each and roll the same.

It can be very attractive in one's narrative to replace the given with the leave. Because if I equate my foundational circumstances with the leavings, the discard, the refuse—even the ruins—of others, I feel more entitled to use them, to build from that rubble. Spite proves an effective mortar in the early part of one's life. What I put in play, I keep in play.

In those lessened stakes, my play—my life, my self-serving self-making—is among other things a *reply*, even a *remark* on the human abdication that got me here, rather than the fulfillment of a promising endowment. If *the given* suggests God, grammatically, or some illeity or other (which Emmanuel Levinas traces in the everyday French and German existential clauses *il y a* and *es gibt*), *the leave* likewise betrays a mystery, one to live out more mortally. That is, insofar as the given is loosely interchangeable with *the before*—apriority—the leave is likewise a duration and its fixed metaphorical field, more specifically so: In the game the leave begins when and where you see a subject forming, or subjectivity transferring, a subject in play again only when and for as long as addressing the setup. *No one* is there in the interim, but it's active: it turns from and then turns to.

I mean, the magic act of the leave is that gradually, motion-lessly, the frozen scatter of independent entities are reorganized into relational possibilities along a single-point perspective, a subject position, interpellating the new next agent of the game, calling him to stand where he needs to be. A priming that delivers him to his cue. Eventually—it has been in early middle age for me—you find that to answer is also to resume and, in resuming, to reconcile with posterity. Queer it if you can.

On Confoundedness

Permitting Shame, Error and Guilt, Myself the Single Source

My grandfather, my mother's father, Jimmy Lee Goard of Patrick Springs, Virginia, whom all five grandsons called Papa, a giant gentle heavy-footed man, a barber and a mail carrier and a farmer and a veteran of the Second World War, hardly spoke at all. So it was all the more startling that there was a word he sang when he said it—rarely, when assessing on the spot something that "beats all" one has ever seen: *Caaww-on-found!* The middle note lowest, as if let out on a swannee slide whistle. The mess, for instance, that two tag-team-wrestling nine-year-old cousins could make of their torn carnival-size stuffed animal opponents and the basement furniture was worthy of the exclamation. More melody than utterance, the word was for apprehending a moment out of control, one boy balancing *in flagrante* still on the "turn-buckle" shoulder of the vinyl sofa. It sounded wonder short of rage. I never supposed it meant *damn*, but I guess I knew it was an acceptable Christian expletive. My cousin Craig and I knew we were in a God-fearing, God-loving household.

I'll bet I learned that one could be *confounded* to Hell in the hobo-baroque Edward Dahlberg novel *Because I Was Flesh* that I savored in my late twenties—where I also learned the words *priapism* and *prepuce* and *cuspidor*—rather than in the Milton I was assigned (and never read) in college. Dahlberg's prose has King James cadence with a hitch in its stride—Shem and Ham might wander among the syphilitic and feckless alley vagabonds there in his dusty unpaved early industrial Kansas City. Where Dahlberg inhabited the perdition of the damned, *Paradise Lost* only further mystified Old Testament cosmogony and Holy Trinity theology, elaborately annotating it all, in pentameter verse no less. I was the first of the Goard family to graduate from college, and at Chapel Hill I was much more inclined to skewer and outpace the predestinarianism I grew up on than to amplify and investigate the abstract machinations of the messenger angels and the fall of man. It is however in Milton more than anyplace, in his pandaemonium, that the two primary meanings of confound are conflated. All my childhood and youth I thought to be confounded meant only to be confused. But I knew the hell of it.

To be confounded is a condition more distressing than to be confused. In confoundedness, the bottom has been obscured or has fallen out altogether. Clarification may yet be an antidote to confusion, the confused person understands, but the promise of bewilderment's finitude, the basic assurance that "this too shall pass," has dropped from confoundedness. So it is a form of suffering. In the early part of my life, I got myself into this state frequently, I found myself lost in it: in school as the youngest in my grade despite delayed reading readiness at home, with other boys in tests of masculinity or allegiance, in the mysteries of my parents' disdain for one another, and in the more fearsome moments in the church meetinghouse. It would begin as a small vexation, an inability to keep up with the lesson, to find a foothold. This would give rise to a rapidly forming certainty that the presiding rules and demands of the situation were understood and satisfied by everyone but me. Ergo: all rules, every demand, any situation. The swift, plunging anxiety that my inadequacy was detectable was overwhelming and isolating; and if I couldn't fabricate a plausible way to disappear from view, then when my panic *was* noticed and public exposure grew probable, I strenuously suppressed and—failing that—muffled the breakdown into tears and great gasps for air. At that point, my senses stirred into a chaotic whirring, the outside world receded into a muted terrible scene, everyone turned to behold what was draining away, and I could only watch behind a shaky, watery scrim. Recovery was often protracted: the mental playback of a remark or grimace could reactivate the humiliation. It was bottomless sometimes. I think this describes the routine annihilation many troubled children undergo. My affliction, it would seem, was particularly acute. I remember being angry at my mother, who, when I called her at work to report that I was home from school and had locked the doors behind me, would ask me everyday and first thing, *Did you cry today?* I hated that the question should be asked, a dull reasonable question and a stinging torment; I hated that I lied; I hated that she could tell; I hated that I couldn't explain what was wrong, ever; I hated that I preferred no one try to help. My frequent silent meltdowns were certainly my most salient social attribute the summer before fifth grade.

My cousin Craig, my exact age, was the younger of my uncle's new stepsons; they had built a house nextdoor to Grandma and Papa. Craig was the reason I was privately excited that I was to live with my grandparents the summer my parents divorced. We were alike somehow. They said he was having a "hard time" with the adjustment. He heard the same about me. They stood us back to back to see who was taller. It varied. We'd roll our eyes and run off together again. Sleepovers were easy, and when we woke one might ask the other how much looser was his tooth today. We made cardboard championship belts, we tagged one another in, into the match we contrived always to end in a pile-on, the result of avenging a lowdown attack on one's partner. Do you believe in godsends? We were almost ten. The comparability of our situations, like our bodies, brought us into relation; it was our family's wish to express it even, press us together, heel and calf and butt and blade and crown. At the end of summer when my mother picked me up, they said I was to be man of the house now, whatever that meant. I wasn't emotional about it. Riding home the three hours south on I-77 I had a new sense of wellbeing; I had found some firm ground beneath me that was mine to return to, no matter where I was. I closed my eyes is how. I was on his mind too. I had come across.

For a long time nothing went here, in this essay, which is trying to locate its subject. What is absolute answerlessness anyway? Is it like a dark *place*, whose contours I am sounding? Is it a kind of *guide* appointed to tour the mystified through the premises, keeping much concealed? Or both, the way Chaos in *Paradise Lost* is an area of Hell *and* a figure presiding there, who aids Satan's designs on Earth. That way.

Confoundedness and revelation, waywardness and prodigal return: these are the primary components of the Primitive Baptist personal salvation dynamic I grew up in. The first parceled pair, which holds the active ingredient of deliverance, the fountainhead of the faith, cannot be sufficiently unpacked for its content, except in abstract figurative language that is inherently exclusionary; so it is expedient that the other pair—its vehicle and apparatus—is offered in *narrative*, with great inclusive appeal to sentiment. The story is a version of the very oldest story: a homecoming. Invariably it takes determinative shape from the subject's incipient wandering and temptation. Then, suffering and wretchedness; then, asking forgiveness and mercy; then, with surrender, acceptance back in the fold; communion; and then the promise, on the sunny margin of that distant shore, in a city bright and fair: palms of victory and crowns of glory, reward in heaven by and by. So: within the story of homecoming, further in, inmost, another homecoming, the transformative one. At ten, twelve, fourteen, I understood where inmost was, and was honeying something trustworthy there; but I hadn't been shown by God, as had others who knew the invitation after the sermon and singing was for them. The story broke down there for me, and became something unforthcoming, alienating, non-narrative. When they spoke of the transformation, the activation of rebirth, there was nothing more to follow. Just words. *If there is one among you here today. If He has reached down and touched your heart. Ready to answer His call from on high. In robes made white with the blood of the Lamb. Find your name written in the Book of Life. If it be my portion. Take up your cross. Take His yoke upon you. Make your burden light. Receive His Grace.* The phrases used to describe the key transactional operations of revelation and salvation seemed always in their sanctimony to displace and defer the goods and, in their high-rotation currency, lost their value even as metaphor.

What a cruel time for poetry! When the stakes couldn't be higher, when one wants to *know*, as I did, past analogy, how that which is grounded in him by "mortal encumbrance" can take flight, how a light gets lit in him that cannot be extinguished. Primitive Baptists preach a strict Calvinist anti-missionary doctrine: salvation through faith and not works. Critically, the strength of your faith *is* your evidence that yours is one of the eternal lives purchased by Christ's crucifixion, and life brings many tests of faith. Your place has been predetermined. You must wait for your call. If it comes, you shall know from a new, keening assurance of His grace that you are one of the chosen children of God. If not, not. Deliverance remains a black box confounding to those who are thereby rendered still in the dark.

I watched my mother get baptized, a couple dozen feet out beyond the bottom plank of a half-submerged wooden staircase down into a dark green pond, in water hip-deep, in the countryside outside Monroe, North Carolina, in the mid-1980s. Her head was rested in the hand of the preacher, whose other hand raised the Bible, from which he proclaimed. She was wearing a different dress, plainer and coarser than the one I had sat beside for hours that morning. Her heels and the preacher's shoes and socks were by the water's edge. Much was sensible. Her immersion was performed with a frightening violence and a simple, sodden beauty I recall, and the whole ceremony was barely audible from high on the banks where I stood with the others, too shaken to sing with them the hymns they knew to sing and without hymnals in the sunlight and open air after. I hardly knew where to look, grateful that soon she was returned to the car that had driven her separately from church. I was afraid that something would have changed in her when I saw her next, when we were next alone, and I was more afraid that nothing would have changed. An older woman, a sister, saw that I was standing alone, upset. She asked me twice what was wrong before speculating aloud that the holy presence of God may be working on me too. Listen, she recommended.

I think the word *confound* first appears in the Bible in *Genesis*, several generations after the flood, in the tower of Babel episode, when God sends an angel to scramble the one language the sinners use into many, so that they may not understand one another. It was and is this way for me, talking with a devout Old Baptist, even, primarily, my mother, who on the topic of faith can suddenly lift off out of the register of one-to-one communication into the highly stylized phrasing I recognize twenty-five years later as church diction. As if one were speaking and began suddenly instead to sing. *A closer walk with God. In such a way that would be pleasing to Him.* The effect is to seal off thereby from further conversation, to seal in self-certainty. Even at forty, I revert immediately to the vexed child I was, and with some resentment on his behalf, who wished to hear but only overheard the words. *The path of righteousness. Tho oft have I strayed. Set aside worldly, fleshly things. This veil of tears, of strife and sorrow, trials and tribulation. Take Jesus into your heart. Keep one another in the fear of God. She is asleep in Jesus.* I preferred the prose. Sinners drawn down the aisle, each towing his story behind him, each then turned to face us all and testify.

As peripheral and extreme and old-world as it seems now to most, the redemption narrative I grew up with is a deeply American form, more dependent on abject darkness than on enlightenment, pre-requiring from each presenting prospective member in his public profession of faith a testimony of supplicant unworthiness, valuing most the lustiest stories of self-destruction and weariest misery and even greatest reluctance to forsake adult secular pleasures to come home like a child to simpler origins. Now, in a certain mood, Bob Dylan's version of "Can't Go Home This Way" or Ray Charles's "Goin' Down Slow" on *Crying Time* can totally overpower me. I am a sucker for the examination of pride in one's last or lowest moment when the return home—now or never—equates with admission of misguidedness and failure. Their situations, and so their lyrics, are similar enough to be outgrowths of the same folk traditional. "I was young when I left home / kind of been out ramblin' round / and I never wrote a letter to my home" so "Somebody please write my mother / and tell her the shape I'm in" because "not a shirt on my back, / not a penny on my name / Lord I can't go home this a way" until "on the next train south / mother, you can look for my clothes home / and if you don't see my body / all you can do is moan." Men becoming sons again. It may be prodigal return is my greatest fear. I quite understand choosing death instead.

At my grandmother's funeral in Patrick Springs this April, just three months after Papa's death ended their seventy-one-year marriage, the preacher, himself unwell and short of breath, stepped heavily to the pulpit and began by reviewing how he had known Jimmy and Elaine personally. He said that their sweet and precious, often wordless way with one another, the welcome he felt in their presence, and their simple faith had been part of a validation he had felt years before in returning to the flock, after the long divergence he glossed not so briefly for us, full of sin and prideful, lonely low places. He swept his tobacco-yellowed silver hair back and wiped his face with a handkerchief, and it seemed he was crying just recounting it privately. Momentarily, he appeared confused. In the front pew with the other pallbearers I did not know, distant family, I was moved by his homecoming and the personal unworthiness he established for himself as qualification to continue. Then: Sister Elaine is *resting, saved, asleep in Jesus,* until *His return to take her home.* It is a sorrow of mine that there I too shifted, in a need to contend with his phrasing, translate it into some that worked with my own spirituality, and fend off an inappropriate consciousness of my alienation from the gathering.

Outside my dwindling family of origin, I am known, if I am known much at all, as a poet. One might even say, a poet's poet. Though less baffling the stronger I grow as a writer, my work is not especially welcoming to the uninitiated and one can feel excluded there by a somewhat nuanced consciousness of literary tradition. The poetry in my two books has been fairly assailed and praised by keener readers for three salient characteristics: its peculiar (unless you prefer naïve) blend of abstract, postmodern impersonality and the discernibly autobiographical; its verbose musicality, beholden most to the music of the sentence, the complex and resourceful sentence; and its flashes of bodily, sometimes sexual (and then only homosexual) physicality. I am all too aware it can be rather a lot to take on. Unlike some contemporary poetry, it does not abandon deliberateness in its fondness for discovery. I suspect it is in that way contemptibly willful: it seems to care to connect, to share, to land, but it will not be direct except as one of several modes. It tries on aphorism but will not arrive at epiphany, preferring a moment-to-moment revelatoriness, which celebrates the spark and fire (merely) of poetry itself. I have recreated, in essence, the immersive experience of enigma which so repelled me as a child. I imagine it is part of what makes me confounding to the people who knew me best as a child. The two members of my mother's family to whom I have come out as gay have not apparently shared this information with the others; but my career as poet they know enough to remark and be politely rankled by. From their perspective, how is it that I might come back from something like what I became?

Yesterday, three months after my second book, *A Several World*, was published, in which time it has been reviewed only sparsely, I received a letter about it from Douglas Crase, an older writer I admire. He accounted his experience reading the book straight through, letting out a "whoop," he says, by the end, at a particularly transactional moment when a train hopper and his beloved aboard already, the one reaching to hoist the other up into the moving cargo car, seem to switch subject positions, *your eyes holding heaves of mine*, so that the chase is then made by the one who had been braced against the palettes. The tramps *make it reach* and seem to ride on deeper into the more and more magic night. He said that reach, erotic and spiritual "where sensuously appropriate to Earth," connected for him several times throughout, remarking that finally he found in it qualities of Virgil that had made that poet's work a kind of home for him. It is the best and most beautiful letter I have ever gotten about what I do. In bed before sleep I'll admit I too read my book, first time since it became a book, as he did, because he did. I finished as he said he had. To come across again.

The night before the funeral, in the same single room of Moody's Funeral Parlor in Patrick Springs where the service would be held, I stood, receiving the respects of my grandmother's church friends, between my mother and my aunt Barbara. A hundred times awkwardly I traded "thank you" in return for *She's better off than we are.* I was mistaken regularly all evening for Craig, whom I haven't seen in years, but whose beard must be brown and blond and, okay, gray and whose eyebrows must be heavy, and hair a little tousled, strategically where receding and thin. Also: "You stand alike," one woman said. Craig had been able to come for Papa's funeral and presumably had worn one of the six plastic carnations when I couldn't. Now the inverse. As it happens Craig had had an accident that day—was fine, at home in Atlanta, though his car was totaled. His girlfriend would have to drive him to work, and so forth, until he could afford another. Barbara seemed unusually unnerved and said he "just couldn't seem to get anything started." I recognized the language from how my visiting professor jobs had translated to the family over the years. Craig was the second Goard to graduate from college, soon after me, and had done well by my measure and, despite a dark and distancing adolescence, was teaching fine art to high school students, and had recorded a couple of albums as a drummer in southern rock bands. Barbara slung her arm around me every time I was misidentified, sweetly offering, *No, this one is Sandra's, he lives way off in Arizona, but we'd claim him if we could.* Each of these hugs was, for her too, especially poignant. At the end of the night, she wanted to take a picture of the phenomenon, and I stood for it, but it didn't come off; she couldn't capture the similarity everyone had seen. It eluded us.

On Abstraction

Permitting Shame, Error and Guilt, Myself the Single Source

At some point in a poetry writing course, with developing writers reading and producing poems, I find an opportunity, even a kind of necessity, to pause and address abstraction. Usually the moment is for a kind of facilitator's intervention, to acknowledge an exasperation with a ponderous poem, or else a gauzy impressionistic one. I come in as someone to validate the exasperation, to sit with it, maybe offer a way out. Even to say "abstraction," to behold it as a quality, involves an essentializing act of abstraction: the nomination of a categorical type to which *an abstraction* belongs. Love, peace, flight, desire, terror, corruption, symmetry, chance, death, appetite, primacy, doubt: these are of course abstractions. Opportunity, necessity, exasperation, nomination: abstractions. Shame, error, guilt. Abstractions are hard to avoid. Language, or at least a Germanic language like English, which is built by and for our productivity with it, seems designed to turn *reticent* or *quick* or *believe* or *complain* into nouns, the better to contemplate them as subject or object, to propositionize about them as concepts or forms. Like places or people, anything that can be isolated in its nominal state can thereby be made a player.

The play, I have insisted to class after class, is important; here is an area where burnishing the language is possible. Error might lean in to Appetite and ask, will you introduce me to Complaint? Reticence might wait all evening to make her presence known to Desire. It doesn't take much to suggest allegory, to excite a kind of turbulence in the atmosphere of language, to refract attention into a stereoscopy or overlay of realities. I have concocted assignments to write, for instance, the script of a real lived incident,

81

but with the attendant abstractions cast as the only "characters." (The stage directions are often where the poem emerges.) There is, I invariably muse aloud to my students blinking back at me in this weird training, a kind of attunement to everyday uses of abstractions in which we can hear or infer a sort of theater. *Shame prohibited Publicity from disclosing the expenditure sooner. With every step, doubt was stirring up terror, and finally we had to admit we were lost.* It is usually the case that this sort of talk precedes some reading I have photocopied, from Laura Riding or Emily Dickinson, as far back as *Piers Ploughman* and as far forward as Kenneth Koch's *New Addresses*, in which capitalized abstract entities (Truth or Patience, or Jewishness or Carelessness) are given actions and interactions to perform or are addressed by the apostrophizing poet.

Rummaging through the foot locker or the four-drawer file cabinet by my desk would uncover a number of these stapled sets of poems on whose cover pages I have written, How to Do Things with Abstraction, or Abstraction and What to Do with It. That handwriting is in some instances eleven years old. Within some of the handouts are press releases produced by NASA for its Mars Rover missions, in which—illustrated by action shots of the two named remote robotic vehicles—Spirit is said to investigate Desolation (a crater), or Opportunity, to draw down its final energy reserves, for instance. Somewhere in these files, too, a few remaining laminated cards I more than once created and distributed to students (and friends and confused love interests who accepted them as gifts), with a photocopied portrait of Peter Mark Roget on one side and on the reverse in small print a columned list of the first 178 categories, the abstract relations, in his thesaurus. So this has been a touchstone of my teaching. But what is it I have tried so hard and so long at?

Partly I have meant for these ludic devices and overdetermined compilations to uncouple *abstract* and *concrete* as poetry's supposed toxin and antidote, or to cant the plane into a field that may allow for poems that are both abstract and dynamic, both abstract and material. There, that. The "materiality of language" is a term one hears in the company of poets, and has meant little to me; hearing it, it's hard for me to imagine anything other than the rounded humps of m's and n's or the rivers of text down a page; it makes more sense to me when I consider Dickinson in particular. When in Emily Dickinson "Detour" is stood as a noun, or "Release" or "Pause," it seems reinvented, or so refilled with potential it spills much of its more common definition. It is as though she has sited a place where value has gathered, where value gravitates. There's a radiant energy at the word. I do have the sense of the word stirring awake and participating in the formulations of reason and subtle sorcery she is articulating. The circuitry is charged. "My father—that Pause of Space," she writes in a letter, after Edward Dickinson's death. A coin is set spinning there. A talent.

Finally the gain of all these exercises I have proctored and all this intermittent study is not some honed facility with concepts as agents—and in truth some of this clever poem play with students has trivialized the unnerving power in Laura Riding and in Dickinsonian metaphysics—but, rather (I admit), a real, steadily building, learned conviction that there are spirits, *numina*, in language. That, specifically, a substantive where it consolidates a kind or a quality under a name, a noun, is drawing on, or *raising* something like a god. A god being that spirit which obtains in a certain situation or petition, which is dormant or dispersed before being called and brought into operations. Is a god substantially different from its summons?

On a plinth in the desert courtyard within the cathedral complex at the 350-year-old Mission of San Xavier del Bac south of Tucson yesterday there was a loose, laminated prayer card to Saint Anthony. The long day's sun was softening a small splotch of candle wax that had fixed to it. Part of the prayer reads, "I implore you to obtain for me." Anthony is the patron saint of lost things, just as Michael, I think, is the patron saint of suffering, and Thomas the saint of doubt or conversion; and saints are not gods, but like ancient Greek deities they are propitiated or invoked or consulted when their respective purviews and specialties are pertinent to the believer. Love and Sleep and Valor and Dolor and Wisdom were gods for early Greeks, not yet intrinsic to what we now call the self; they were sought and summoned to apply to a human circumstance, to oversee it. "Obtain for me" seems not only wonderfully humble as a request, but also similar to the content of a polytheist or pagan prayer. It is also the writer's wish when selecting a word, when letting a line or sentence take hold and establish and act in relation with what else precedes or comes.

When named, the entity—Bone or Habit or Election or Treasure—enters into council with the other capitalized imports in a Dickinson poem; each presiding over its invested constituency, together they situate the axes of the poem. The poem is reread, and relationships across syntax develop and conspire with the syntax, or query it. Emily Dickinson did not capitalize every noun—maybe about half of them; the selectivity and idiosyncrasy of her method is a living moment of the philology she studied. In Dickinson there is a revival, a late uptick heartbeat, an atavism: even among American writers, who were generations late in adopting the protocol in English to capitalize only proper names, Dickinson held to an old fashion, and made it hers. Never was a writer a custodian of language more than she. Capitalizing all substantives, however common, was, for a time (in Samuel Richardson's correspondence, say, circa 1700) a standard practice, and before then I think concepts and nouns of significance were capitalized as an author saw fit, when he or she felt they were entitled to superordination, and in register it wasn't substantially different from personifying concepts. When positioned as antecedents they might be referred to as she or he. These are the ghosts in custody still. If you ask me, a paganism lived through the monotheist lexicons of Medieval and Renaissance literature, lived through Neoclassical and then Romantic moods, when lowercase prudence became customary. For a measure: the 1850 version of Wordsworth's *The Prelude* has far fewer named nouns than the 1805 version. Little s shepherd. Little c conscience. Big n Nature. Value added.

Siting the place where value gathers. Calling what's there by the name of what obtains there. (Calling to mind, calling by its name, calling into being what's there by the name of what obtains there.) How do gods form? Is illocality their address from the start? Here is a speculation, a scenario: Perhaps there is the bend of a river, bright under the sun, where waters accelerate, and the fishing is good there, or life itself feels quickened at the spot. At night it is frequented by moose in estrus. A special place. Generations understand the luck of the site, the propitious fizz above the rocks, and the moss it makes on the banks there, and over time it is a place one visits to ask for a turn in fortune. Something like "fortune" or "flux" or "tingle" becomes its handle. An abstract. By its handle it can be drawn, like any word, anywhere; the visit can be virtual. The word is drawn thereby into prayers, poems, into speech. Eventually, far from knowledge of the bend of river, one comes to host the visit of the word when it obtains. Something of the moose and fizz is preserved in it, belonged to it.

It may be *belonging to* is the raison d'être of these numina. As in the Mission, which has a designated alcove before which to behold each saint's beneficent downward gaze or ecstatic upward one, there are offices for Paternality and Subsequence in Laura Riding's long poem "Memories of Mortalities." She names the fixed values in the math she makes of her childhood, sickness, and schooling, the poem's three parts. Laura is drawn last into the play, through the "slow grammaring of self," to exist among the familiars and genii. They pool and consolidate and adhere to their physical hosts. My experience bears this out, and I am no visionary. Back from the Mission, I believe I can tour my house as if carrying an instrument, a theometer, say. I feel charges sitting here.

When I lean back in my chair I can just see the corner of a white cardboard photo mailer envelope under my desk. The foot locker of teaching materials rests against the one of the back legs of the desk. Beside the other, in the corner of the room, this envelope. It fell back between the desk and the wall down to the floor about ten months ago. I sweep around it when I sweep. Inside there is a photograph, of my ex-boyfriend Doug as a child. I believe it is a photo of him in costume, in bright tights, dancing and acting on stage in Fort Worth, no older than ten. I won't look at it again. In it he is hopeful and springy and eager to please, and also surrounded somehow by sadness or hurt. Soon after John and I moved to Tucson I found it; it dropped from of a book—*The Sighted Singer*, by Allen Grossman. I was relieved, as it had been a point of contention with Doug; in the months after we broke up four years ago he said it sickened him to know that I had this last of the childhood photos he had given me, and angered him that I had misplaced it—as though my disinterest in sharing our whole lives had won out in this material way. I bought the envelope right away and intended to mail it to him, knowing that was just, deliberating about what note if any to include. Under the desk delay and regret and irreconcilability have gathered, and even after I mail the envelope and clean up, there they will obtain for me. Please, irreconcilability, accept my surrender. Be germane, that's all, amen. I believe, all the way to his Silver Lake mailbox, in your charge.

On Peripersonal Space

Permitting Shame, Error and Guilt, Myself the Single Source

Peripersonal space, or near space, is the entire volume of space within a person's reach, or within a single conceivable momentary extension of his person. Think da Vinci, and the geometry of his jumping jack in extremis sketch. All that. It includes then everything at arm's length, and a bit more, in a pinch: in a car, for the driver, peripersonal space extends perhaps to the push lock on the passenger door, should the next moment at a stoplight present an unwelcome stranger approaching the vehicle. There is something potential, temporal, contingent about it. It feels insufficient then to call it *space*, to measure it in cubic feet. It includes the accelerator and brake pedals and the bag of groceries that one might shield from forward propulsion during an urgent stop, as well as the imagination of those events and immediate responses: stop and shield. The windshield wiper and the front wheel well are not part of the driver's peripersonal space, near enough but accessible only by a *series* of steps.

In dance, peripersonal space is called the kinesphere. In compositional improv among other specific practices, a dancer develops awareness of her kinesphere and that of anyone or anything that may enter it, attuning to opportunities for interaction: synching, mirroring, dovetailing, clashing, chasing, et cetera. It is not wrong to call it a body's gravitational field. In the audience attending such a performance, you might feel the tug in your own near space, as two well-attuned bodies pass one another. Little empathic ecstasies, solar flares, brought about by their transit. In that seat, I have reached out before.

I was driving in Los Angeles when I first heard of peripersonal space. I was on surface streets, returning from teaching my class,

87

Life Writing, at Otis College. It had been a good class; I think it was the week we had read Claudia Rankine's book-length essay about surviving the first term of the Bush administration, *Don't Let Me Be Lonely*, a kind of emptied-out everyman account of four years anyone might've endured, and I was buzzing from it. *Science Friday* was on the radio, with Ira Flatow, a segment featuring an interview of two psychologists, joint authors of a book which laid out the science behind a new formulation of selfhood. Together they built an explanation: the self was not just the corporal body and the sensate, sentient being in its form; it was also everything within its immediate orbit. The soccer ball behind a person's heel or the toggle switch on the nightstand lamp beside a person, even in the dark, especially in the dark, are experienced—in their potential for interaction—by that person as part of him or herself. As constituent of the self as a knee or the bridge of the nose. It seemed an extreme theory, ethically troubling, yet also very compelling, satisfying. In fact the example to which the authors resorted for illustration was the one inside the slowing car. A bag of groceries or a passenger in the seat beside the driver is perceived as *part of oneself*; to wit, securing its wholeness and safety in a sudden stop involves not valuation but rather instinct, to protect not what is most precious but what communicates itself as an extension of the self: the loosest, heaviest things in one's near space. That which is most susceptible to detachment from the intact integer one feels one is. I may have remembered the study so well because I was training in movement improv that spring; but surely it also imprinted on me because the authors, who shared the same last name and the same title, both of whom Ira addressed throughout as "doctor," were, he eventually revealed, mother and son.

Since I began this project, I have tried a number of times to write about my mother and me, and have abandoned a few attempts already. If these essays are, in part, inroads to disinhibited autobiography, as I have come to claim they are, and demand they be, I feel the imperative to address the subject above all others. But ours is a relationship so deep and damaged and (still) so tenuous it has defied emergence. It might be best to begin simply, in a gesture, as anyone, anyone in the passenger seat shielded by his mother's outstretched arm. I was a well-protected little boy. My mother was instinctive with me—nearly animal—inclusive, attentive, loving, and largely unreflective. As a child I was just the same.

This driver-passenger seating arrangement was ours, fundamentally. If we were seated side by side, in a pew at High Hill Primitive Baptist Church—or Union Grove or Spoon Creek—or in a booth on the rare occasion we ate out with my father, Curtis, I sat always to her right. I internalized her concern that, because she is left-handed and I am right, we would bump elbows. Sitting close, two-bodied, our outer arms would each cut the sirloin or hold the hymnal. Invariably, in public, we were told that I was the spitting image of her, that our resemblance was uncannily close, and it was true, bothersome how self-evident, we looked and acted alike. In those parts of North Carolina and Virginia it was called *favoring* her. Fair-haired, high forehead, pale skin, slight, soft features, big teeth. Sensitive, awkward, quiet, reticent, easily embarrassed, apparently guileless, quick to cry when made to feel inadequate or slow. Even without her, living with my grandparents the summer my parents divorced, each of my grandmother's friends, approaching me, began, *You must be Sandra's boy.*

On our own at home, I remember much tenderness early on. I think my emotional fragility, my inconsolable bouts of overwhelm at school and my inability to know or to say what was the matter, determined that I had no close friends; and though she was popular at work, my mother was lonesome and lost in her first marriage and its aftermath. We had each other, we would often say to one another, if we had no one else. We survived on $35 monthly grocery bills (the smell of Vienna sausages would

89

not come clean from my lunchbox), and I helped her pin sequins and tassels on styrofoam ornaments when she had no money for Christmas gifts. Many times she told me that I would find in the long run she was my best friend. And reciprocally, when she would say, as often she did, that no one loved her, I was quick to protest, to offer myself, an exception, her only sunshine, in the song. She prized my sweetness and attention. We played another game on the carpet in the den, a game she had discovered first with our dog Arnold. When she knelt facedown, in what now I might call child's pose, and covered her face, and pretended to cry, the puppy would also whimper and manically search for an entry into the fortress of her hurt, licking her hands and pawing and digging the carpet for access. One evening she began this performance but we both knew Arnold was outside. I took his place, nibbling solicitously, relishing the tacit invitation, giving pleasure with my worry. I learned I could reverse the roles and expect the same. My crisis, my frequent and inexplicable loss of composure and attendant shame, presided over the game; we were rehearsing breakdown and empathic despair. The game stood in for actual help: an expression, really, of remediless suffering. She could offer only that I was like her, (in my fortress), that we suffered the same fate, that our bond prevailed.

It is more than embarrassing to relate all of this. I come up against the inappropriateness of, for one thing, sharing what is only half mine to share. But is that partiality, expressed by that proportion—half of one—ethical, or healthy for a grown man? Roland Barthes has famously said that to be a writer is, essentially, to violate a primal taboo, to "play with the mother's body." No. I love Barthes and he is a signal influence on my conception of this very book; but the remark presumes a class and level of literacy I was not born into. (How self-betraying here to pause to avenge my mother's unsophisticated heritage before I continue divorcing myself from it.) Language eventually was for me, rather, the realm that provided for the rejection of that body, and for drift beyond its orbit. My facility with it came via the man who married into us. From their weekend away, they brought the proposal home to me, and I too said yes.

Throughout my adolescence and young adulthood—that is, the entire duration of my mother's second marriage, until Frank's death last year when I was thirty-nine—our relationship was characterized by the dissolve of that early intimacy and marked by several disruptions and mutual cancellations. Individuation. What can be a normal stage of development was for us already delayed and then protracted by the constant airless terror in her abusive marriage and the business of evading its seizures. My rapidly necessary independence was weakly managed and—when noticed—very nearly peripersonally troubling for her. The persistent empathy I have gravely felt throughout and despite has been a source and site of deep anguish.

When I was thirteen, soon after their marriage and his adoption of me and my transfer to private school, Frank, my mother, and I visited friends of his in Denver—a former Justice Department colleague, his wife and their older children. The first evening, after dinner, we broke into teams to play Trivial Pursuit. It was 1986. Before long everyone was remarking my cleverness, earning green and yellow and orange pieces of the teen team's pie. I liked the wine-drunk repartee. When my mother asked a question of her opponents, arts and leisure, they answered with quick certainty, *Eydie Gormé*; but without hesitating, reading again the back of the card, she insisted they were wrong; the answer was *Eddie Gormes*. Frank and the other couple, all of us, laughed, realizing her error confronted with the exotic spellings, and they teased her, piling on in the easy, witty, high-bourgeois way she wasn't accustomed to. Her humiliation was instant, and only I could see that, trembling behind the pillow she had bravely brought to her face to feign laughter, she was not going to regain composure. I knew what she felt; this was me a thousand times before. After an uncomfortable period, the pillow was lowered, she spat her terrible, hot, resentful hurt in a burst, ran to the bathroom and did not reappear to the group until morning. Sandra? Mom? The door stayed closed. The game, the evening, the trip, was over. So was the dynamic of my childhood. Because her condition would be stunned, stagnant, unsupported, whatever further distinction I attained would be distinction from her (what happens if there are two Pygmalions in the fantasy, one more adaptable?), and whatever self-determination I asserted would be for my mother a betrayal.

It was as if inevitable. Soon enough, I would walk out of my mother's church, sit in the passenger seat of the car in the hot sun for the remainder of the hour, and never set foot in the building again. I was fourteen. The sermon was about the righteousness of women who accepted their role as helpmeet, meek and shamefaced. I had seized a moment to make irreprovable my quiet protest, then: not on my account but on my mother's, weeks after the sermon in which Brother Larry had locked eyes with mine, explaining from the pulpit why man laying with man was an abomination. It was becoming clear most of the world did not accredit my invisibility as we arranged for it at home, the more different I grew. Suffering a traumatic marriage and in an ideology that abhorred me, my mother continued to find no way to witness me—let alone create a holding environment without judgment for the person I was in the turmoil of becoming—and so we deepened a merciless old pattern. If I could not be sufficiently seen, I could be surveilled, I could be watched for signs of something; and to avoid detection, I could withhold, avoid, deceive and cover. I could keep out of reach.

Inevitable, too, then, was a situation we assiduously forestalled for some time. At seventeen, caught off guard by daytime television, a talk show underway about gay teens, I watched, with my mother, two boys kiss, while the live audience catcalled and laughed and grimaced. Where was the remote? My peripersonal self must have been exercised—da Vinci jumping jacks and then some—seeking it. She remarked that she didn't understand how or where such people proliferated. I wielded a statistic: it was likely that one out of ten of her acquaintances was gay or lesbian, and left the room red-faced. Minutes later, she found me downstairs, stood on the landing, and fixed her gaze on me, her jaw tight. *You'd better not be gay*, she said. Privately devastated, I believe I managed only sarcasm. *What a nuanced and thoughtful philosophy of parenting you have.* Such was the condition and extent of our mutual alienation and impasse. There was not therefore another opportunity for candor with her until I was twenty-three, in 1997, when she and Frank visited me in Brooklyn, where I was finding a rich if complicated new context for my sexuality. Suffice it to say, about the confused half hour of nearly wordless, fearsome emotion ending in Frank's insistence that we all get ahold of ourselves, that it did not go well. She has not visited any home of mine in the seventeen years since.

The mother-son coauthorship of a book, any book, particularly in the field of psychology, and especially at a vanguard understanding of the self in relation, remains perverse to me. I can hardly conceive of it. The separation necessary to decide independently to come together and collaborate with the person who successfully, unilaterally claimed you and your body as part of him or herself, on a book of objective science about the purposes and means and limits of such claims in the construction of self; to be able to count on and work with his or her understanding of individuated separation in healthy human development: this was for me beyond what could be contemplated. It was the publication of my first book, *Not Even Then*, when I was thirty, in fact, that demonstrated how unthinkable a mother-son harmony of authentic selves would be.

My mother did not take my first phonecall, more than a week after I mailed her an inscribed copy. Frank, to whom I had sent a copy separately with an inscription even more (hideous to me now) reflective, answered the call and said that they were dismayed, that she was beyond words, that the book was unforgivably inconsiderate of her. He was incredulous that I was astounded. The book, like many first books, was part bildungsroman, contained a poem performing my consternation with Primitive Baptist salvation logic as well as an elegiac portrait of my mother seeming to vanish in the dewpoint steam where I had watched her work one morning; but largely the book retains a poetics of impersonality, thriving on the anyone/everyone account that lyric poetry customarily finds. That was in fact a quality described by the blurbs on the back. Bodies of men are in it; desire, love, alterity, the New York cityscape and North Carolina landscape are reckoned in it, fugitive, mostly unattached to person. *Para*-personal. Regardless my mother's reading of it was penetrating. When she did take my call, she told me in a terse voice that she was disgusted by the book, which she found so offensive and shameful in its "display" she wished every copy could be retrieved and burned to ashes. She repeated herself, making the wish. She felt her religion was ridiculed in it, and further prophesied that one day I would be prostrate before my God begging forgiveness. The publication had been the highest achievement of my life to that point, and its warm reception—in national review attention—was plunged by the most basic and complete of rejections. To pretend it didn't matter, to project that I was untouched by her curse, their disapproval, was poor strategy, especially as I consented to their requests to join them at Christmas and to return for Frank's illness and surgeries. First time I did, six months in, soon after her dog died, I was shocked by how my mother had aged. Her weight gain was ample, her hair was lifeless, she wore nothing but sweatshirts and had dark circles under her eyes. I believe she had suffered a kind of nervous breakdown. When there, I could tell it was useful to her I was out of my context, hard to see.

My best friends were not wrong when they gently advised that one doesn't necessarily need to maintain relations with someone who is ashamed of you or who erases you or who will not agree to meet your partner or who covers the truth in conversation with others, just because she is your parent, or just because she is hurt. Nor need one ever return, they said, to the constant trade of humiliation and misery in a toxic household. Eventually, as many as five years later (I can admit now), I recognized that my resistance of that advice was itself a form of knowledge. There was a way to align myself in right relation; to develop at least consciousness of feeling, even at thirty-six; to practice healthy limited relationship with someone with compromised capacity; to openly acknowledge to her what is hurtful or unacceptable to me; and to heal, which would mean a refusal to conceal or be concealed.

The most intense confrontation we have since had arose one late night a month before Frank died. Wobbly, heavily, he came to the kitchen and sat down on his stool, witnessing with some amazement the quickly escalating conversation we were having, about behavior I found unacceptable. She was alternately enraged and distraught for hours as I patiently and intently repeated how I felt, vanished and disrespected; if we were to have a relationship going forward I would insist on greater fairness in our mutual toleration of the other's worldview and I would not disappear part of myself for her benefit. At one point I blocked her swinging arm from striking my face and stepped back out of slapping distance; at another I needed to say aloud that I was not a part of her, and she needed to cry out that all she ever wanted is for someone to love her. (Frank needed to ask, rhetorically, to cover the wailing, what on earth it was she wanted from him.) Some several minutes later, we shared a long pause, registering what we all heard her say: *I shouldn't have to choose between my God and my son.* It was I who suggested there was room for her to be openly, publicly honest about who I am and still disapprove of it, equally openly. She forbid me to use the word *God*, and I forbid her to use the word *lifestyle*. This seemed a bit of useful resolution. She needed some space, took a short walk, which is when Frank said, for the last time to me, *You're a good man*, and went to bed.

In the weeks after his death, my mother told me that during an argument a few years into their marriage, Frank accused her of engaging in incest with me. Why she told me I don't know, but I remember the night Frank had pointed out, as illustration. They had returned from their honeymoon in Hawaii, one of the first nights we spent together in the new house. One of the 1986 World Series games had just ended, Red Sox and Mets, on our new TV, exciting. At bedtime, as a kind of prank, or in a goodnight hug that wanted to be prolonged, I had crawled under the covers with my mother, in their new king bed, in the filtered rosy light of total envelopment, and nestled against the side of her body, as a surprise I suppose for Frank when he would return from the bathroom and peel back the bedspread. I may even have said Boo. Was the picture unseemly, a thirteen-year-old and his thirty-four-year-old mother lying in an embrace—he in his shorts and she in her negligee—or a gross misjudgment of new family playfulness? Did I think I might be tickled, skedaddled? I remember his pause—*Jesus Fucking Christ!*—and his slow, stiff retreat back down the hall, we so much more lithe than he, and then the look my mother and I exchanged: *Uh oh*. Maybe a giggle? She said she was furious with the accusation, and told him I had only been a boy, just an unsure boy who worried he was losing his mother, and was hanging on despite all the disruption.

On Dossiers

Permitting Shame, Error and Guilt, Myself the Single Source

"I am merely opening a dossier," says Roland Barthes, again and again, throughout his three final seminars in Paris in the late Seventies, each course posthumously converted to a book, each book divided into annotated weekly lectures, subsectioned into brief semi-independent scholia. More than lecture notes but short of sustained essay, each book is agile, esoteric, and unsynthesized, pivoting continually to consult yet another tangential text or discipline. In my favorite, a course he called *How To Live Together*, Barthes unpacks a kind of fantasy he has (and so do I) of *idiorrhythmy*, by which the editor says he means: historical or utopian arrangements, at some remove from civilization, wherein individuals live singly but with common spaces of voluntary, nonfamilial togetherness. For examples, Barthes sees fit to make brief forays into the Shakers, Thomas Mann's *Magic Mountain*, the history of the university, and certain Greek monastic traditions, signaling throughout his express intention to pull or recall only what he wants, to forestall exhaustiveness, by repeating that he is only glossing, *opening the dossier* wherein much more lies, should anyone wish to pursue it.

A dossier then is a repository of otherwise loose relevant material, a file, on a subject. Usually a human subject. The term is professional, and may be primarily legal. I believe there is even a kind of briefcase called a dossier briefcase, one which—in my image of it—is still portable by a handle but larger than standard, with overtop flap and front clasp. One might keep a dossier on a client or a suspect, or, in other professions, a recruit. I think it has currency in the world of espionage. For me, though, for many teaching writers, more than ever, the term is a codeword of academia, full of a kind of consternation for those who struggle for a career there. As I write this, it is again high season for applications, and I am yet again updating my teaching dossier, which has been kept on file with a dossier service since 2005. In a practice I began last year, I have copied and pasted a few appealing job postings—a meager amount this year —from a horrid site called Academic Wiki Creative Writing 2015, a kind of toxic message board in which anonymous posters, who identify themselves and others by their credentials to measure in shorthand their relative professional attractiveness ("2 Books, PhD" or "1 book, MFA, visiting position"), carp at one another, speculate about each search's fairness, and hiss at the opaque system generally. *Who do you think you are, shitting on a TT poetry job at Purdue? You'd be lucky to make it past initial screening for a Big Ten MFA program. A huge name will get this job.* The wiki has so many pop-up ads, it crashes my browser if I am on it longer than five minutes. I move my cursor around the window so I don't hover over anything unintentionally. I feel certain each time I've caught a virus there.

Not long ago a dossier was understood (if that's the word) to be "evidence of teaching success," evaluations from one's students and peer observers, syllabi, and even sample assignments, as well as letters of recommendation from more established writers in the profession, letters invalid unless applicants waive their right to read them. Applications are now so numerous, that amount of material would be prohibitively unwieldy and so schools request only the letters, until finalists are named. Still I pay the service $65 a year to keep my three letters unknown to me, and mail them to the search committees. As do, I presume, the majority of my 267 fellow applicants—the number named in the rejection letter from Rice University last spring. The rest of the dossier one provides himself, later in the process, at the preliminary interview stage. *Dossier, from the French, for "on one's back,"* I have started to say in shorthand commiseration, to my confrères on the outs. A family, we, of unaffiliateds.

Last season I was lucky. At the Modern Language Association conference in Chicago, I had preliminary interviews with five schools, more than anyone, everyone said. I bought a suit bag to contain my new second suit, the overcoat I purchased for my first such interview six years prior, a few shirts and all five ties I own, as well as a $400 flight and a $225 registration fee, as it is unclear whether one is admitted uncredentialed to a conference hotel; my own room was $150 per night. A week thereafter, Rice was the school that called me back, for a campus visit. I was one of three candidates flown to Houston and put up in a chic boutique hotel, and elaborately hosted. I toured the campus; taught a sample class; interviewed with more than a dozen faculty members, including the dean of Humanities and the chair of English; shared four meals over two days with would-be colleagues; and gave a presentation of my work. The job went to a fourth candidate, an "inside hire," time would reveal, the lecturer whose closed office was next to the one I had been given as a staging area. It made sense of the unnerving disengagement I had perceived from the faculty who torpidly attended my late-afternoon talk, and of the odd *c'est la vie* air from the chair as she was confiding to me that my teaching materials were the finest in the search. My dossier was exceptional. Thanks.

I am merely opening a dossier here, on disappointment with academia. The file is rather full. I have been second in line for three other tenure positions at universities, and in each case I have been told afterward by someone in the hiring department (once by telephone with the express assertion that he would deny it to the end if ever I reported it was he who told) that the job was "rightly" mine were it not for: first, the dismissal from one search committee of its own chair, a drinker, for violating confidentiality with another candidate—he had been my main supporter;

then, elsewhere, the eleventh-hour capsizing of my candidacy by a poet on faculty who protested the committee's recommendation with an elaborate, persuasive denunciation of my work that he distributed overnight to his colleagues; and, last, the veto of my selection by a dean who cited other needs in the "opportunity hire." (It wasn't a year for queer.) Nothing entirely nefarious about any of these situations. In each case, someone qualified got the position, and anyway I am not foolish enough to believe academia is a meritocracy. But hurt and cynicism have, for me, compounded the basic demoralization of spending the effort against such odds and in a climate with so little transparency. There is a one-year master's program in Geographic Information Systems where I live, and there are jobs for graduates. I will not repeat behaviors and expect new results. I *like* maps.

Executive summary of my professional situation is a practice I would like to break, a practice that belongs (like a physical memory) to two recurrent subjectivities: the letter of application, in which for years I forecast my intention to "narrate and detail what is merely glossed in the attached CV," an importunate phrase that now makes me cringe, and infrequent but regular conversations with my stepfather Frank, each time conforming to one seeming objective: to present fully formed, self-aware, undeceived, but upbeat and particular about possibilities on the horizon. He would reply with a broad flat question: *Tell me, how is it that one teaches poetry?*

There have been two questions—in the many warm emails and congratulatory phonecalls—occasioned by the announcements this fall that my book had won a significant American poetry award and had been "longlisted" as finalist for another even more prominent one. The first, many times over, is: Well, doesn't the job market look quite different now?, and the second, asked just once, by my friend Claudia the night of the heady awards ceremony, on our walk back to the hotel after dinner:

Is this the sort of thing that means anything to your family? It's the former that triggers a kind of panic. In truth, I have always felt, and it is a shameful sort of narcissism to feel, that others—while saying some version of "surely it's your turn *now*"—hold a secret understanding of me as a rather sad, unfortunate figure. Is it my hair? Is it my unnaturally thin wrists? Is it my somehow sorrowful face in profile, its misguided, expectant smile? Is my voicemail gay? Gay enough? Is my posture unemployable? And it's the second question, certainly the more tragic one, the one Claudia asked, that kindles, alternatively, a sturdy kind of peculiar strength in me, which I don't think is spite. Implacability is power in my family. That night her question was occasion to explain that Frank had died, and to acknowledge aloud that with him alone (who routinely bought prize-winning books) the import would have registered. With my mother, no. She seems glad enough to know of my achievement but is (rightly) dubious, as it never seems to parlay into livelihood. Appropriate to our history, I never offered to send her a copy of the book and she hasn't asked for one. At some point Frank, were he alive, would have found opportunity in my presence to explain to her why a National Book Award nomination was a big deal. I can hear how that would sound, and that is not something I want. But I can't think of a way outside of our triangulation I ever learned, while he was alive, that he was impressed.

If *proud* is the better word, it would mean he felt an association with, or stake in, what he admired. I think that's something both parties sense, like love. We didn't love each other.

Like many self-destructive people, Frank was largely self-made. In turn he admired above all a bootstrap independence in others; and he shared his own (at one time substantial) financial success pointedly where he sought to level the playing field for the hardworking but not well-born. In my teenage years I was to be that sort of beneficiary. When Frank met me at age eleven, before the dossier on Brian Overby was sealed, it was not a promising profile. I had read *maybe* one book through to completion. I covered my large, crooked front teeth if I smiled, and between my high, heavy twang and the mumble endemic to early male puberty, I was often incomprehensible. I could not (and would not) hold a fork correctly. My best friend Tobby and I were weak and weird and intimidated in our giant junior high and clung to each other in a syrupy brew of righteous revenge fantasy. Primarily due to redistricting, I had been in six schools by the start of seventh grade, and had never had a gifted or interested teacher. My father's very young girlfriend was beating her five-year-old son at my dad's apartment during weekend custody, and my mom and I were scraping by without his alimony or child support. She was wallpapering her bosses' homes for extra money. On Sundays I wore a clip-on tie to High Hill Primitive Baptist Church, and on New Year's Eve I listened to *The Country Countdown* on my mother's blue bedspread all the way to Barbara Mandrell. What did I have when I had all hundred hits tabulated in pencil at midnight? 1984. I was a quiet, private, careful boy. *Sensitive* was the word. I guess he agreed to take that on. I can remember thinking that Frank's adoption of me was *my* decision to make *him* feel included. As I practiced in my old room my new signature, its big new double b's, its bunch-up of consonants, some of which I elided (still do), I had very little concept that he was affording me a different future than the one facing me, or that there was any future at all staring me down. Gratitude was, in the rough ride of our new life together, a hard thing for me to access, and a dicey thing anyway with someone like Frank; it bespoke a dependence, for one thing, which he found shameful if it endured past a certain point. Certain to whom? I gathered gradually that finding my own course outside of his expertise and influence, expecting nothing from him, would be safest. Safest from what? What did I fear when for nearly three decades I dreaded being disowned?

Not fatherlessness, not exactly. It was to that dread I belonged. It was an association.

Though he was a tax attorney and though of course he had confronted his mortality for years, Frank died without a will, without attesting anything, without naming anyone in his plans, so the property he owned alone (not jointly with my mother) became by default the "estate" that my mother and I were to inherit equally. There were a couple of condominiums (a rundown place in Florida that had belonged to his father, another in Charlotte he lived in before he met us), a 1957 Pontiac Star Chief he had partially restored, season tickets to the 2013 Charlotte Panthers home games, some seed investment in a struggling Italian restaurant, and several other smaller concerns, all of which we quickly realized we would need to liquidate. So before I left Charlotte for two weeks in Palm City to repair and clean the Florida condo and enlist a realtor, we needed together to make sense of the dozens of hanging file folders he kept in the several drawers in his home office, and separate out the useful records. Our inspection of course had collateral effects. It confirmed a number of dark suppositions for my mother, and profiled a downfall I had underestimated. I assembled a sort of paper trail of his diffuse and involuntary retirement from his law firm. He was edged out as his diabetes and disability inhibited his productivity and he lost his hard-won (and hard-driving) impunity and career-long leveraged advantage over other attorneys who then drew him into conflict and outfoxed him, denied him pension even in the end. His home office became a private and even abject place, a mess, where he learned how to email without a secretary, tinkered with investments and lost a great deal of money day-trading (five-sixths of his wealth, best I can tell), and wrote long, rhetorically impressive, morally stinging, logically airtight letters to officials at Bank of America (who denied him mortgage refinancing) and insurance claims adjusters, who were likely not as upbraided as a reader worthy of such prose would be. There was a file for 1935 SW Silver Pine Way, Unit H-1, and for 310 West 10th Street, for each property or investment; a file for medical receipts and claims; and a file for each of several pro bono cases on which he had remained a consultant. Each concern had a file, and several were duplicate, redundant files he had apparently misplaced and started again. There were a number of files, for instance, called "Nixon Portrait."

Frank had purchased in the mid-1990s one half of an oil portrait of Richard Nixon. The dossier was richly detailed. His partner on this venture was a former girlfriend, a lobbyist in Washington named Mary Scott Guest, who apparently understood that then Senate Majority Leader Bob Dole wished to hang the portrait in his office; the painting once purchased was immediately loaned to Senator Dole. It could be assumed that it would rise in value as its new quarters deepened its provenance. The artist was a South Carolinian illustrator and painter who had been commissioned by *Time* magazine to paint the portrait in advance of its 1972 Man of the Year issue. Ultimately the editors ran a different cover image of Nixon, as the portrait was rejected for making "too penetrating a comment." As it happens, it was the second such rejection; the first artist they approached was a sculptor whose bust of Nixon had portrayed, they concluded, "too sterling a character." This was documented in the typed letter the artist's representative had written, which I found in facsimile twice before I found the original as well. Perhaps the real portrait here was America's slow-forming image of the self-made self-saboteur they would soon reelect. Together Frank and Mary Scott had paid $25,000 for the painting. My subsequent research revealed that the painting sold for only a few hundreds at auction a couple years ago, by an anonymous seller, to someone in Charleston. The dirty sale established the current value of the painting and no action against the auction house would be worth attorney costs. I got as far as trading messages with a docent at the Nixon Presidential Library, before seeing, as it were, my fruitless intel collection in the mirror. It's my hope it is the artist himself who recovered the work.

Closing that file and opening any other, an inventory would similarly reflect on the times, but it was hard not to feel that the files' reflection on the man was a paltry late snapshot of a life that exceeded them and was mocked by their arbitrariness. Where was the file on Frank's role as student bar president, a progressive, at NYU Law School in the early Seventies, surely the most turbulent time to be a student leader in the history of Greenwich Village? Where was the file on his rough Irish Catholic childhood in Ridgewood, New Jersey, whose contents would give context to his tortured expression whenever in the presence of a certain stern-faced older man in the childhood photos I found loose in his office? Who was this man who had stepped in after his father left? Where was there a file on his first years in the South, his absorption into aristocratic families in the home he made of Augusta, Georgia, as a young lawyer, after serving at Fort Gordon during Vietnam? What would be revealed in a file, if there were one, about his key role in the acquisition of several failing Texas banks that led to the formation of NationsBank? Could something there help explain what he did to exploit an environment of Reagan-era bank-deregulation at the end of the savings-and-loan crisis and discover the loophole in the federal tax code that helped CEO Hugh McColl's Charlotte bank become the behemoth that would be Bank of America? It had earned him one of ex-Marine McColl's signature crystal hand grenades for a job well done. Where was the file on his participation in the Aspen Institute Roundtable on Law and Society, at the invitation of Justice Harry Blackmun? I remember well when I, by then in Charlotte Latin School and fully alive in the literature we were reading in Honors English, found Frank carrying from sofa to bathroom not Scott Turow but Herman Melville's *Billy Budd*, which Justice Blackmun had himself assigned to all participants. I read it too. I never told him.

In the bottom drawer, in what could be called inactive files, one almost went unnoticed, one of the thinnest, a file on whose manila tab was written, in Frank's unmistakable hand, the words *Brian Blanchfield*. I pulled it. Inside were three items, all of which I now have with me in Tucson. Item 1. My revised birth certificate, post-adoption. In North Carolina, it is or was custom in 1986, apparently, to supplant the biological parent's name with the adoptive one. *Curtis Overby* is nowhere to be seen on the document, though it appears to have been issued in 1973. Indication is that Francis J. Blanchfield, Jr., was in the Winston-Salem hospital room, age 28. Item 2. A photocopy of the front page from the local section of a *Durham Herald-Sun* from February 1993. I can remember one of his colleagues had sent it with a note that made mention of Frank's legendary Super Bowl parties at the bar near his bachelor condo. The photo there showed me sitting on a platform in a tree in the campus forest in Chapel Hill. My hair is long, swept over my ear, and I am wearing a jersey-sleeve shirt and swinging one booted leg in tight jeans. I would have been nineteen. I am holding open a heavy paperback and soaking in the sun. The caption reads, "Keeping the Peace. Brian Blanchfield, a sophomore from Charlotte, reads a copy of *War and Peace* as he perches in the Forest Theater at the University of North Carolina at Chapel Hill. Temperatures climbed into the seventies on Super Bowl Sunday." Item 3. An essay I submitted on October 11, 1994, to English 58, my Shakespeare class my senior year. "The Legitimacy of Don John the Bastard, in *Much Ado About Nothing*." An A paper. With pencil annotations by Professor Megan Matchinske. A study of the play's malicious outcast villain born out of wedlock as a plain-dealer among much scrutable seeming, and his portrayal as homosexual in the Brannagh film. Nietzschean genealogy of morals stiffly applied: ill-doer as symptom of societal disease.

It is possible I showed the essay to him, which would have been risking quite a lot simply to share something I was proud of having written. I don't recall. Reading the essay in his office, I felt myself split. I mean, I would need three dossiers to keep this artifact. I can remember well who I was writing it, on my blue-screened Brother word processor, up late on ephedrine after my Pizza Chef shift in my little apartment at 107 West Main Street, while my first boyfriend, Austin, twisted in the sheets on my futon bed. We would have met a month before, over a barrel fire at a party (our marshmallows touched). I resisted his beautiful body until the end of each paragraph. Is there pleasure greater than that sweet agony? Then, now, with eleven years' experience as a professor myself, I know, too, the perspective of Dr. Matchinske, who recognized there a rare urgency in undergraduate analysis and pressed its author for substantiation and concluded that I uncover more questions than I answer, but good ones. And, I can begin to see how it would have been significant to Frank, a moment for assessment at the end of a decade. As the newest of the three items, the last, it may have occasioned the file and collected the scatter of other material retroactively. Probably last of all he wrote on the tab the words of my name.

★ ★ ★

The office the hiring committee at Rice had given me to prepare for my job talk, like each of the others along the hall, faced out onto a row of magnificent live oaks, each one wearing a rugged tinsel of Spanish moss. I closed the office door and sat down at the desk. On the other side of the door the airy, light corridor led around variously to the modern building's smart mix of aviaries and courtyards and well-lit meeting areas and caucus workrooms. Architecturally it structured, it seems to me, an optimistic, exemplary idiorrhythmy. Each scholar in her private quarters with a singular concentration, and a trade of ideas in the common areas.

I wonder if Barthes had this ideal in mind, in his last academic appointment he didn't know would be his last. My nerves were building as I looked through the notes of my presentation—when I was frozen, of a sudden, in the gaze (for how long had it held me?) of a downy owl deep in the branches of the oak, studying me. Something stirred in me, and I thought of Frank. Why do we say *brought* when we say *brought to mind* when *sent* might be the better word? What I remembered, and chose that moment to recall as blessing or sanction or something, was the last night I saw him, late, after a difficult conversation of unprecedented openness with him and my mother, a night when I moved from needing to know where I stood to wanting to stand on what I knew. It was a turning point that is very nearly a trope in father-son relationships. I saw him see me. As if for the first time. Not so much approving as noting for later use the way another person was managing his struggle. That night, I had in a dream the most serene and safest sensation I have ever experienced. I was lying on the firm ground on a very dark night, away from everything, in a kind of breezy clearing in a forest. The dream had only one moving actor, a great bird of prey, an owl, I somehow knew, in silhouette, dark against the darker sky. From a great distance off, it glided, very few wingbeats, in absolute silence, and was impossibly large directly overhead. I was below. It knew. That's all. It condoned, and sailed on. And I felt an extraordinary peace.

After I returned to Tucson from Houston, but before I received the letter from Rice, my friend Aisha listened to my story—to which I had added the lucky detail John and I had learned, that Rice's team nickname is the Owls, if you can believe—and recalled that in some aboriginal faiths, encounter with an owl means that someone has been designated to die. She looked it up. It was foreknowledge she said, a farewell. A real gift. Why had it reappeared in Houston? I don't know, she said. It seems like you already have what you need from it.

On Frottage

Permitting Shame, Error and Guilt, Myself the Single Source

I can't bring myself to rhyme it with cottage, but I've heard it pronounced that way. The French pronunciation makes it sound like a delectation, a frill or a whip, a froth. Anyway that's the one I say when I say it. I don't know when I first had the word, or whose word it was, not someone I did it with. I know I was doing it without a word for it, and with men who didn't seem to have a pre-established idea of the thing or its name, young men doing what comes naturally. Put their mouths together in a kiss and between their bodies no room for daylight. Some men magnetize. That much I know. But this is essayistic foreplay.

I'll bet it's used capably in one of W. H. Auden's louche and randy poems, those that came to light after he died, but probably not in any by e. e. cummings, who by contrast enjoyed being known in his lifetime for them. It feels appropriate to their shared era, particularly the rarer backformed verb, to frot; but, the attendant divide between their sexual orientations marks an area where disagreement lingers still about the definition. It seems primarily among older straight people that frottage is understood to mean a sociopathic, furtive rubbing against strangers in crowded places, like subway cars. (Masher! was the cry in sitcoms already long in syndication when I was young—followed by a customary whack to the head with a heavy purse, whereupon over the laugh track the hapless innocent taken for pervert stammers his explanation.) As it happens, furtiveness (I'll claim it) is one of my defining attributes, and much of what I miss about New York is the erotic charge of returned glances in crowded places, and even the brush of intention where accident is a cover. I have leaned back yes into

109

excessive leaning. But frottage, to gay guys I know, has nothing to do with that.

Frottage is a rather broad category of consensual, nonpenetrative, (usually) hands-free sex wherein both optimally naked bodies press against one another frontally (most often), and genital stimulation for one or both is an effect of rhythmic movement along the vertical axes of the bodies. If the two are no longer standing, verticality is remembered in the movements the bodies find, to climb and slide on one another. Up and down rather than in and out, as a general rule. The term encompasses a range of contact. Between two men, two erect dicks pressed together along their entireties, to the very bead of the frenulum, is one way, at the high end. Here are happy, thudding imprecisions. Or, further down, one guy's dick along his partner's upper inner thighs, or pushing up into or behind his partner's scrotum, where the prostate distributes and multiplies sensation, somehow also canceling it at the same time as it will. May this be a gloss on the word *intercrural* if they're still using that clumsy confusing term in Sex and Gender in Antiquity courses that furtive college boys take as soon as their schedule permits an elective. (Those of us once reliably seen farming the HQ 700s of university libraries.) Frottage, as a term, is not necessarily specific to men with men; it's also a kind of sex women have with women; although *tribbing*—similar in principle I think (including on principle its variability)—and *scissoring*, missionary or otherwise, are terms not shared by cis men. I'm not sure what along these lines men and women do together, though I think *dry humping* is still a term in use, which begs the question. To what extent is frottage, or whatever wordless thing we do with one another and have done for millennia, understood as *simulating* penetrative sex? To say it is derivative of intercourse discounts the draw it has: one follows his and his partner's pleasure there. But as pleasure builds it's not unusual for one to say to the other, *I want you inside me*, or *I can feel what it would feel like to be inside you*.

It was at first a surprise to me at twenty-two, and then a kind of—like sex itself: repeatable, singular—discovery I came to expect, that the partners I found (finding me) in New York were, same as in North Carolina, rarely expressly into penetration. What did we solve (a metaphysics, a phobia?) each time we made our mutuality exterior? We met each other there. Sometimes we marveled to each other in the excited dark that we should have found a fit like this, that we were called to this, that if before tonight there had been a script there was with each other a thrill in ditching it, that our sexuality even had ever been—we further coaxed each other—*all about* contrariety; and the new exploration of the other's body and the body's new otherness seemed endlessly potential and plenty ecstatic. How little the rest of the world knew!: ever the cry of the lover. All four *longer* relationships I had in my ten years in New York excluded anal sex altogether. Perhaps it was we were relatively young and our bodies were for the most part (as a type) lean and super-responsive, hyper-sensory, and so topicality was deep enough. In young men's bodies, surface is spring-loaded, underfitted with a nervy meso-layer ribboning everywhere between skin and skeleton. Any friction is already double friction, since in the confrontation flesh against its own frame hosts much of the sensation. Likewise, in frottage an important distinction is underscored: unison is ineffective. Two-way is the way of togetherness: response compounding release seeking. Low long vowel at the ear: approval. Tops of the feet beneath your partner's soles bouncing him up onto you. Does it break the spell to wonder whether strong ankles were of similar use to Socrates, after the banquet, to Lincoln in cold cabin Illinois?

Here's the thing about that time that doesn't seem transhistorical. Easily half the guys who had been strangers a few hours before we were all gossamer with busy reciprocity in our underwear said or else heard me say, in an early pause, catching our breath or resetting to attune to the ambient moment and our wants: *We don't have to do anything.* The opening for disinclination was the space of intimacy. As hesitation, it often functioned anyway as aphrodisiac; and as pass, password. You're like me. We're okay.

In the same year, 1996, New York saw more deaths from HIV/AIDS than in any other year of the epidemic, *and* regular daily dosage of AZT and other medications (together known as the cocktail) was determined a lifesaving protocol for the walking ill and infected, if not too far fallen already. Neither fact would be evident—or believable—until much later. I arrived in June, and found the gaunt, unsteady, depleted men fifteen or twenty years older than me populating areas of the city much as I had imagined them back in North Carolina: aged far beyond their years, lost inside sweaters far too large and occasionally insufficient for the purpose of concealing the sarcoma lesions that emerged anyway at the neckline or cuff. That summer Thanatos and Eros was an intersection quite as real as Christopher and Hudson. The tragedy selected me from central casting to cross their paths; I was functionally necessary to complete the tragedy, in fact. To elicit in a man a glance and then from somewhere his instant reproval of that glance, interest stanched at first flicker, renounced altogether (an apostasy on these streets), or else transmuted to raw resentment, even dark prophecy for the fresh, healthy arriviste. A few times audibly: *fuck you.* Wasting is a late stage of AIDS and is also, or was, an effect of some of the antiretrovirals in the cocktail. Some of my good friends today remain in physiques close to their condition when they were among the first possible survivors. But it was a long time before I could connect to men of the generation I unconsciously insisted was different from me and mine. It was first (only) in books I knew the concept *queer tutelage.*

Does any fifteen year-old ask: what is the maturation endpoint of my sexuality? Where is this thing going, this burgeoning attraction to—in my case—other boys? Is there someone out there who has arrived where I want to be? Can I visualize lasting fulfillment? No. Mostly the future he imagines is fantasy's subjunctive version of the present, were the beloved here now next to me with his impossible eyelashes, snug jeans, and quickening smirk: what might happen. But in 1988 extrapolation had a heavy tug on otherwise sexy contingent if/then calculations. It was grave. I mean, mine was a generation like ones before and after that deeply, darkly valued the category *faggot*, which organized like a lodestar all nascent masculinity, choreographing in any room or gym or field how far from one another we stood, and pulled the tides of our tactical moods—from furious to laconic. But in 1988, if you privately understood you were gay and were capable of basic logical continuity, you had made the further implicit equation between your own attraction to men and the depthless suffering of AIDS victims stranded in their crisis on the nightly news—and not just their appreciable agony but also their leprous toxicity. Regularly, reports stressed their reckless, even willful communication of the virus to others. Sex between men that resulted in infection was in certain instances prosecuted as murder and manslaughter, and men were maximally sentenced for aggravated assault who spat on HIV-negative cops. For so much lethality the American imagination needed monsters to blame and to fear; likewise, to justify the paternalistic hard lines that might be drawn to keep its children safe. The corruption of the young innocent was to be avenged—until the moment he seroconverted, whereupon he too was hastened into villainy. Many of the men sick in San Francisco and New York were dying disowned by their families of origin. Programmatic mass quarantine was debated, and camps—camps—were publicly contemplated. It was at the end of the Reagan presidency when some gray-haired senator proposed in an appallingly reasonable tone an emergency measure to tattoo the buttocks of all HIV-positive men as a "warning" to potential sex partners. I can recall Tom Brokaw managing the phrase "tattoo the buttocks": an indignity to him, one felt. America beheld in its mind's eye for a moment the firm young ass unwrapped, quarry somewhere of the sodomite whose predation would be foiled by the guile of the state. Let me be candid: I had no better (and no less prurient) idea than anyone around me what "counted" as gay sex, and had no knowledge *in my body* of what I wanted from the other body I wished were here with mine. But that news came within weeks of the day I ceased in my autoerotic life the ludicrous rationing bargains I had made myself with regard to images of girls instead of boys. I remember in the complex acceptance a feeling of immanent *correctness*, in consigning myself to a short life expiring on one of these iconic cots, abandoned, ravaged, fouled, destitute, panicked, eyes listing in their bony orbits. I was what I was; it was in me already.

I never had a sex life without having a status. The two were inextricable. My early fantasy of partnership was in fact sealed fast by HIV: if finally you and he were infected and allegiance followed whatever tearful forgiveness, it seemed to me you could not uncouple, conjoined in the blood. That was my gay marriage. The brave intimacy, and then hurtling undead together through the newly meaningless trappings of the world, liberated by the worst once it had happened. I came to realize I shared this with a lot of guys who came of age in the late Eighties. There was no question but that I would get tested after I became sexually active with guys in Chapel Hill. Three weeks and then three months out, with dread, and then twice a year, was the rule. The first time I came out to multiple strangers was in my senior year creative writing class, in a long poem called "Anonymous Testing," and as I recall it restaged the walk from my apartment to the clinic, distilling an encounter en route with a couple of glaziers, father and son, or rather with their careful haul, a large pane of mirrored glass they had unloaded from their truck. I wobbled in it and waited for it to pass before I crossed. It carried away all the distance behind me, a horizon I had interrupted, a sunny blue day. The clinic had been on the other side. I was negative. (I told Mr. Seay so, when we met about the poem, his rubbings of Yeats's grave above me on his office wall.) I took home a pamphlet I already had and also condoms for me and Austin, and had them on hand for Elliott that once or twice, and Greg usually had his own, but we didn't use them, any of us. We found we didn't much have to. Furthermore none of us were tops or bottoms, or we liked it undeclared. But we knew all the disputed contact points of risk, had a taste for them, and were fervid enough that I often found afterward I was abraded, so I was tested regularly.

I am tempted to read the horizon in that mirror that crossed my path as a glimpse of the late Jose Muñoz's "forward-dawning horizon," his trope for queer futurity in *Cruising Utopia*, a book that would not be written for fifteen years but one that is concerned with the era I was walking in. For Muñoz—among a clutch of important theorists I feel I have been waiting for, Lee Edelman and Lauren Berlant and Jack Halberstam and Michael Snediker and my friend Maggie Nelson—the "here and now" are not the coordinates of queerness; queerness (which for him reaches back to import and include preidentitarian practices before gay and lesbian lives as such) has its own temporality, deferring instantiation and organized by drives other than union and reproductive posterity. *Not now* and *not yet*, these queer drives "off course" or "misfiring," for which frottage is only a marker but perhaps an important one particularly "useless" to forms of procreative increase, in turn can produce orders of relationality that obviate or détourn the traditional unit of family, proposing (if not forming) units more supple and adaptive to the precariat fluidity of contemporary living. That seems particularly true for the lovers I had, artists and dancers and writers (and lawyers and production assistants and parking lot attendants) spotting one another in the late Nineties in New York, encamping for a few weeks in pairs together (or months or years) and keeping tabs on each other's barn-cat semi-independent way thereafter. Recursive and recombinant and (as needed for efficacy) agglomerative patterns might map over time the relations made by a generation of people born under the specter of HIV and raising one another into an unforeseen adult queerness in New York. That we were in aggregate less committed (and more averse) to insertive and receptive roles in sex than the generations before and after us is doubtless a function of the epidemic and the ruthless dithering and phobic hand-wringing policies of a republic we saw leave for dead its afflicted, the dead and traumatized whose mentorship we could have used in Neverland.

We fucked, some of us, a feeling of fucking, felt for the feeling in one another, and got off on it. That was our erotic imprint, a kind of code. The surprise that kept surprising us: we liked loving one another. That was a print we *made*. And we learned the permissiveness of sending lovers beyond the present attachment; after facing off intimately, reading each other to one another as if in replicase, we might then face forward together and take what comes, watch each take it. Each one a piece of me. This (the question of who we are according to what we do) is—I see it now like an historian—the subject of my first book, *Not Even Then*, which would not exist without HIV and which is in several poems at pains, it seems, to disclose a bodied metaphysics I taught myself (and spread?) in the sex I was having and in the pursuit of Possibility to which I was acolyte. Queer world-making is now a prevalent and increasingly useful coinage: a projection of affinities into a system that can and will hold you. Like a brother I am responsible to Douglas and Terry and David and Brett, boyfriends there, and also to Rob and Matthew and Dan and Jason, romances that rooted as friendships and became, each uniquely, part of a kin that includes Annie and Samantha and Maggie and Eliot, all of whom know I would drop everything if they needed me. But

I *feel* that way too about Carvel and Davíd and Vestal and David and Jeff and Simen and Kieran and Shawndon and Justin and Zal and Victor, and Jeremy—brief affairs whose spellbound trade in vulnerability and openheartedness connect me to them. Is it "natural" to imagine, to wish, these are the flashpoints that visit as visions or sensations a last time when I die?

The forward-dawning horizon was especially trembly at first. I had been in New York three months—fewer than a dozen people in the world knew my address and number—when in September 1996 in Windsor Terrace, Brooklyn, I received a call from the New York State Health Department. I was alone. The conversation was quick. I was alone. A health official tersely delivered the news: Justin Lennon (Greg was his middle name) had listed me as a sex partner and had tested positive for HIV somewhere in Georgia. It was urgent that I make an appointment to be tested myself before a date two weeks from then; the result would be reported to both me and the state. With no doctor or insurance (I was working as an office temp), I took the number and the Bedford Stuyvesant address they gave me, and hung up. It was happening. I wasn't yet out to my parents. I recounted to myself each time—eight, nine—that Greg and I had been together and turned forensic in my memory. I planned my next steps. I called and emailed Greg. No answer. His former roommates in Charlotte weren't helpful about where or why he was out of state. But they had mail to forward to him and would give him the message to call me. I had to tell David, whom I was dating in New York. He was distant about it, and decided to stay where he was that night, with his brother's friends in the city, and for the next several days. He said he'd wait and see what would happen, didn't much see why he should worry. The day came; I transferred from the F to the C train, which I had never taken farther into Brooklyn, and got off at Nostrand. The clinic was busy—there as on the train I stood out for my whiteness—and the practitioner I met with semiprivately was upfront: as many as half the people who were testing at that center, even more who'd had phonecalls like mine, were in fact HIV positive, and I should think about my support system. I should return in ten days to get my results in person.

It was very early one morning when Greg finally called; he was keeping strange hours, had been working as a club promoter in Atlanta. He sounded weird, stoned, exhausted, or just remote, and told me that he hadn't been with anyone since me and since he and I had been exclusive in the months we were together, he had concluded I must have infected him. His tone sharpened; he didn't want to talk anymore. That was it. During the emotional freefall of the next several hours, for a second time I discussed my status with an older straight poetry professor. Michael Collier was my first advisor at Warren Wilson, the low-residency writing program I had just begun—we'd completed just one exchange of poems and commentary. He read rightly the distress in a note I had sent and called me from his home in Maryland. Whatever else he was doing in his life that day, Michael spent a half hour listening to and gently advising a rattled and isolated young man sorting through (and finding the words for) the sex he had with other men and with what frequency and precaution, teasing out the logic of contagion. I felt his concern. I mostly held it together until he asked if my parents knew.

The day of the trip back to Bed Stuy was a crucible, some kind of parable in danger and courage. After the transfer, a couple stops in, two young men about my age stepped separately into the C train, and stood facing each other at opposite ends of our car, hurling threats, spitting invectives. This was the end of a chase. Within a few seconds each had drawn a handgun and their voices began to rise and even to shriek. Their rage was full of real, mortal fear. Many of us on the train began to look down and still our movements, as if any of us could disappear. I think they would have killed each other had an older man in the middle of the car not stood, between them, speaking to both with his hands outstretched, alternating his eyes' attention, balancing. He must have been seventy-five, hair entirely white, his face bumpy with black freckles; in a sure, even voice, he began to tell them what was going to happen next. He conducted them from the middle, insisting as the train was slowing for the next stop that the man at the far end get off the train, save two lives if not more, and just walk on. He did, and when the doors closed, the gunman closer to me began to shake uncontrollably. Pin-drop silence until he departed too, onto the next station platform. I followed him off. It was my stop. The results were waiting. I was negative.

Greg, too. I found out weeks later, when he returned more of my calls, his test had been a false positive. The blood bank had been mistaken. Georgia and New York stood down. The worst had happened and then had been undone.

I went on undoing it. Did you?

On Reset

Permitting Shame, Error and Guilt, Myself the Single Source

A couple nights into a housesitting stint in my friend Eliot's studio apartment in Brooklyn one winter, I tried one of the video cassettes he had said were blanks, on which he said I could record any of his estimable movie collection on a tape-to-tape recorder he had. Eliot is now, some fifteen years later, a successful screenwriter (his debut film stars Kristen Wiig and has major distribution this year), and he lives in Pasadena; but at the time Eliot lived a few blocks from me on Flatbush Ave, above a hair salon, and worked as a librarian at ABC Television. He described his job then as the person who presses play, who makes sure the programming is loaded, who interrupts this broadcast during technical difficulties. Anything on tape or reel that belonged to ABC he cataloged and pulled and queued as necessary.

The tape I loaded was not blank. On the screen a digitized clapperboard chopped out the name of an actress, the abbreviation OLTL, some numbers also meaningless to me, and the word *audition*. Take one. *Action*. An executive behind a desk distractedly calls in a guest at the door. Entering what seems a carpeted corner office a young woman, a tall African-American in business attire, emerges and finds her mark, introduces her character to his. It emerges that the executive is interviewing candidates for the position of his secretary. Particularly devilish, metanarrative, for *One Life to Live* to make an interview scene its audition scene, for what would be for both character and actress a recurring role, a hire. The scene is for the character a winning one, short, maybe three minutes of dialogue, a review of her qualifications lengthening into a conversation wherein it is revealed that she has

121

noticed his motorcycle in the parking lot and furthermore can relate knowledgeably, even disabuse him of a misperception he has labored under, about the Harley Heritage Softtail Series. As the scene concludes it is apparent she has the job; none can match the promising rapport she seems to have with him. The tape runs darkly on a few moments until the redrawn slate claps out a new name, the same voice calls *action*, and our attorney again puts down the file he has been examining idly to wave the applicant in. A crisp, attractive white woman, pert, with coifed hair, steps a few paces onto the carpet and addresses the executive. They review her identical qualifications. She has noticed his motorcycle in the parking lot—she herself rides; again he is surprised, charmed, challenged, impressed. If he is a man who isn't afraid of a subordinate's savoir-faire, surely he will hire her.

She is in turn replaced by a third and then fourth hopeful running the lines with the cast member—and more: maybe nine, ten, eleven in all. At the end of each iteration I leaned forward, urging another to follow. I watched the entire hour, then made myself a snack from Eliot's fridge, got my notebook, returned to sit cross-legged again on the bed, and reset the whole thing to play again. Something here was tapping the quickest vein I have, a kind of xylem channel of creative pleasure. Something here I recognized, and recognized wanting, in my own work. It had to do with the change in me it elicited, a reorientation.

In retrospect, the slow moment that interest bloomed into euphoria, more or less at the appearance of the second prepared slate and the nearly identical (but notably varied) play of the actor behind his desk, was the one alive with the understanding that this scene would not have its particular increment of drama developed by another in a chronology. The *development* would be parallel, substitutive, paradigmatic (and not syntagmatic), despite the forward-moving melodrama of the script, of the advancing tape, of time itself. This was a series, a system, a machine run on a simple algorithm—three minutes of banal theater cycled through human interpretation. The banality was not a detraction; in fact it aided the formal pleasure. The machine kept its own time, establishing expectations, the midway arrival of a certain line or choreographed blocking—the lawyer's rising and approaching the applicant, for instance. How would it happen this time? To what, in one run-through, could his hand in his pants pocket be attributed? There was even a word in the script whose relative volatility was a small tripwire to dread; half of the actresses could pronounce the word *implacable* when speaking of their character's qualities: her perfectionism each time would or would not be "implaceable" when she came to it. Repetition trains the viewer of such a thing, until the rules that seem to govern the cycling content supplant the content. One such rule: One of the two players here is dispensable; one stays with the furniture and the script and the square of carpet, and the other by definition passes through. This introduces an ethics, no less than the dicey phrase "one life to live." Hence, another rule: Privilege, positional, outside this circuitry, is a byproduct of this circuitry, watching the secretary reincarnate. The illicit pleasure of screening footage not meant for me was partly in reviewing what each actress could not see: the cheap guile with which she was one of many beheld as if singular by the consecutive executive. Finally authorship itself is reassigned by this structure; if anyone it is the reading viewer, not the screenwriter or show runner or casting director, who has created this art. After all, the whole of the hour of video was not meant as a whole; the auditions were not meant as parts of that whole. The artifice is an effect of their incidental succession, and the call to pattern recognition makes the viewing a kind of code management, the reading a kind of writing.

This is—as many have said in one way or another—the province of poetry, the arrangement of language whereby the sensations of reading are charged with the creative feeling of writing, and vice versa. This is why I reflexively brought my notebook to the television, cued, ready. In an essay I read recently, a poet I admire, Mark McMorris, quotes Paul Valéry as having said something like: the purpose of poetry is to re-create the poetic spirit in the reader. That feels pretty right to me as a real reason I read poetry. Poets often fret that only poets read poetry; but in fact that seems to me inherent to the transactive practice it is. Poetry makes poets. When it happens we say that work is generous. This last year, books by Chris Nealon and Kevin Killian and Jena Osman and Harmony Holiday and Aaron Kunin and Bhanu Kapil were my go-tos. Each of them, midway, I put down and looked up to find the world was changed, a little. That's what I'm looking for, that transfer, a new attunement. In the experience neither poem nor reader has yielded; on the contrary, we generate something together. It's because "a poem is a thinking thing," as my one-time colleague Karen Volkman said somewhere. It's a choice formulation: "a thinking thing," a phrase in which I hear both the poem's instrumentality for thought (it's something with which to think), and its processing of its materials (it's something that conducts thought, as if independently). Especially in books like these—different as they are from one another—where the moves are recursive, where the iterative processing suggests a program, one to operate. This is work about which poets remark, *it teaches you how to read it*, meaning, often, its set of likenesses and equivalences build an interiority as you pass through it. A poem is durational art; but, its running time belies its inclination to reset, to redo. Merely to start a second stanza references the first as a template, suggests their comparability as another track of significance. In the poem or poetic series the repeat of identical sound or parallel rhetoric or syntax or any similar passage or equivalent unit sews a relationship that subtends and subverts the unidirectional *alla prima* thrust

of the poem. Gertrude Stein said repetition is never exact repetition, because the human registering it is different the second
time. For her, the practice has implications, self-othering at
the mark of the selfsame. As Nealon puts it, "my secondarity
achieves a sheen."

A marcher sounds off in tandem with one earlier in formation, to whom he's now attuned. Two pairs of others uncannily
have their ties blown north; they turn in lockstep away from the
rest. Another by himself five rows ahead turns too, though his
tie is tucked. The far marchers in the fourth, ninth, and twelfth
rows drag their stride when each crosses a certain mark. Implaceable. Anticipation tripped by surprise. Again the marcher counts
himself and is answered by his partner. And as the troop moves
through the course, the course is not used up by the passage
through. This is a dance. It is called "The Pangolin" by Mar-
ianne Moore; "My Life" by Lyn Hejinian. *Sonnets to Orpheus.*
"Self-Portrait in a Convex Mirror," "The Glass Essay." Or, recast
the formation: executive secretaries leaving the lot at the end of
the mind.

In John Berger's best essay, one of the very shortest, a small
meditation called "Field," he describes a small squarish weedy
meadow alongside a railroad crossing in France, one at which
he hopes to be delayed so that again he may practice a devotion of sorts. Most times there is no train. But when there is, he
may again look over the field, accustoming his attention, until
something jumps within it. It always happens, he assures himself.
A grackle hopping, a rabbit standing plantigrade. To focus on
the impression it has made is to spot then a second phenomenon,
sometimes tangent, immediate, sometimes in a far quadrant of the
field, a low breeze bowling through the tall grasses. Something
else thereafter, cornflower breathing out a hue in the new light,
some gnats worrying the air in a helix there, the grackle again
hovering for his hidden mate. And then the train has passed, and

the traffic inches ahead. The field is for Berger idling in his Peugeot always a duration, and the field for as long as it is the field is a set of reliably dynamic relations. So, it would seem, is any field, and anything so (squarely) attended might qualify. A canvas, he doesn't say. The essay ends, "the field you are standing before seems to have the exact proportions of your own life."

I brought my notebook to the television. Of course my life's proportions were written there: a secretary (my mother), an attorney (my stepfather), report of a motorcycle (somewhere, my father), a revolving applicant (myself), an embedded standard in the script (unappeasable if you pass, illocable if you don't: growing up queer), and the slate (poetry): one life to live to live again. That is, singularity recast as multiple. That is, one's subjectivity run through by a performance not one's own. Here at the authorless site of my thrill, producing a replacement time in place of time, something expresses in me, the way groundwater is said to express intermittently as a spring. A sense of it having run under all along. "Often I am permitted to return to a meadow," and sometimes the meadow is a soap opera bit part audition tape. The scotched and blotted notebook page I import to the scenario may capture not even the scaffold of a poem but marks the site where "poetry" is anyway reading me, resetting itself, across my lifetime.

It's embarrassing in 2015 not to say *so what* to that and rather to build a trust in those dimensions. I don't say God, but if I'm in a church basement meeting, this is the higher power I let myself conceive. The same way during his occasional interval the field each time instantiates fieldness in Berger, the welling of confluent creativity when it happens draws out my subjectivity and conflates it with my objecthood. I mean, it brings back (or resets the text of me at) prior instances of this influx rush, compounding their current. Something throws forward from other encounters. Seeing dance for the first time, in 1995, Mark Dendy's quick, gestural multivalent "Fire" at the American Dance Festival in

Durham; reading in 1990 *Sonnets to Orpheus*, the first book with a system I understood as inhabitable (though I no longer live there); watching with John in 2010 the Clark Fork River run again over its natural floodplain after the demolition of an old dam in Milltown, Montana. Maybe here are Virginia Woolf's "moments of being" or Wordsworth's "spots of time," (and maybe, too, wishfully, something of Keats's "negative capability"); but in any case, these instances when poetry is cued—forthcoming or not—these sited sensations of renewal coming on, are finally for attuning your own instrumentality, were some other agent playing the thinking thing, something continual keeping its time, in the plain continuousness of your own lived span.

"Choose your poet here," says Muriel Rukeyser, late in *The Life of Poetry*. "Or, rather, do not choose, but recall," she continues, describing the overwhelm of something she calls truth that each person finds in the poem that does it for them, that enacts whatever transfer it is that seems a self-replenishment, "the light of a new awareness that was not something you *learned* but something rather that you seemed to *remember.*" "This," she says, "is the multiple time-sense in poetry, before which your slow mortality takes its proper place."

On the Ingénue

Permitting Shame, Error and Guilt, Myself the Single Source

Heather McHugh once wrote at the top of a poem of mine, in a balletic red script I can still see, *Ambition comes from getting around.* Either she was, true to form, etymologizing in a flash a word I had used, or else the poem I'd drafted occasioned this choice apothegm and she couldn't resist formulating it on the spot. It seemed, once written, like indisputable counsel or perhaps a winking caution. We were mentor and mentee. It isn't untrue, even, to say our mutuality was as apprentice and master. Her letters to me came from her home in Maine, where she sometimes ended her return address in all caps, ME, US. It felt like inclusion.

I was in New York City, living on the ground floor on Prospect Place in Brooklyn, studying literature and pursuing a career in publishing, in which by slow turns and detours I *had* advanced from temping in the science and medical journals division of John Wiley & Sons to research-assisting the Books editors at Salon. com, where because of office space shortage I often reported to work at the Reading Room of the Bryant Park library a few blocks away. Before long, and for three years, I'd be an editorial hand at Farrar, Straus & Giroux down on Union Square West. And on my off hours I did love to get around, to put my body in play, to ambulate the streets of Manhattan. I wouldn't have said I was cruising. It is still my penchant, recalling that time, to loosen want and tactic from my ambition. Readiness for anything to happen itself seems to produce happening. As you go about, the surprise return of Fleet Week or Ash Wednesday turns the year for you; people passing you in their evident customs are your tidings, here again before you know it. And you and yours are theirs,

I suppose. I wrote a poem years later I might have dedicated to Heather in which I "circulate the tender index I am of regularity." Keep moving, they say. In such an education, there is no starting place; it's all milieu. You drop into it and deduce the rules that govern the place.

The ingénue is an old narrative trope, a type. She emerges from a tradition of didactic "slippery-slope" morality tales and attains a kind of prominence in the nineteenth century, I think, corresponding to the industrial rise of the city. Or, at least, the epitome to my mind is Sister Carrie in Theodore Dreiser's novel about the corruption of an innocent in big boulevarded Chicago at the end of the century. Structurally I think the figure of the ingénue necessitates arrival someplace, and likewise the complexity or opaqueness of that place. There must also be the promise that her inherent worthiness shall be recognized and take her far. Hence, most important, there is no ingénue without her counterpart, who extends that promise, the cad—they, too, mutually define. Who is the theorist who attempted a structural poetics of narrative prose? Propp? Shklovsky? I may have these postulates on loan from his charts and tables—so specious a few pages after the slick Russian formalist theories of *poetry*, which more pliantly conforms to system analysis—in my old copy of *Structuralism and Semiotics*, the stiff little black Terence Hawkes paperback primer I still consult and had with me, I can never forget, when in the bathroom at an after-hours club in the Meatpacking District my friend Dan Nohejl needed something to sort the cocaine on. I had never done it before. Is *sort* the word? Cut?

The ingénue Sister Carrie, whatever the tortuous plot of her odyssey from farm girl to department store seamstress to socialite to mendicant, remains for me in the downstairs doorway of her sister's squalid apartment building in her first nights in Chicago, much to the growing horror of her workaday brother-in-law, who forbids her to "look at the city passing by" or some such stammered desire for which she is shamed. To open a backlit doorway onto the dark and busy night is legible already as sex trade. So, the ingénue is defined not only by her antipode, the cad; but also by her opposite, disingenuousness, which motivates the ruin more. It is a cruelty in Dreiser that the least gesture that bespeaks a desire or ambition proves the disintegration of innocence; to continue to present as naïve is insincere, *meretricious*—a critic's word that tellingly has prostitution at its root. The door has been open for men before and after Dreiser to demand innocence as all or nothing. That liminal jeopardy is richest for me, so much so that I can't remember the name or any attributes of the actual opportunist who ingratiates himself to Carrie and exploits her for half the novel.

Ingénue is feminine in French, and the concept is gendered too. A sexually mature, innocent male newcomer to the established milieu without ambition or desire has not been of especial use to literature. I mean the corruption of the impressionable young man from the provinces is a primary theme of European and American literature, has been for centuries, but usually within the form of a bildungsroman, where the rough education awaiting him is poignant because we first have steadily come to know the child—his heroic ipseity, his distinctness—that grows into the man who must navigate the trouble. The ingénue has not *come of age*. The materialization out of whole cloth is unfavorable for psychological development and when male consigns the ensuing endangerment to comedy or picaresque allegory. The accidental do-right buoyed along by circumstance as in *The Charterhouse of Parma*, for instance. Or, the countless fluke absorptions of Charlie Chaplin's tramp into the system, misfortunes no fault of his own. Ingénue refers also to an actress in the repertory who plays the ingénue, for as long as she is fresh. It's best if, in the story, she arrives unagented and gets "discovered."

My friend Ken, a poet and screenwriter, once had calling cards printed for himself (I had one in my wallet for a while) that read, *Ken White. Cad.* And then his email address. The smirk of it—a sensitive young man and his cover—cracks into smile as you grasp that a cad, if there were such a thing anymore, would not self-advertise as such. He purchases himself a complex innocuousness, leaving such a mark. The card, too, is arch. Derived from the letter of introduction, it bespeaks a caste system in which social credit secures welcome and facilitated adjustment for those newcomers who carry vouchers from persons of lateral or higher status. It belongs to the world of Austen, Thackeray, of Boswell on his tour. Johnson in his pocket. Practically, it is what the ingénue could use but by definition does not have.

Ken says he recognizes a tell in my writing and way in the world, performing (even sealing over in) a certain gallantry but pressing harder than accustomed sophisticates do, and also given to self-sabotage in a gouge of candor: a motivational mixup of determined umbrage and reckless faith in language, as if I am set on presenting with the imprimatur of flair alone. Virtue in situ. He too comes from a start in life that afforded him no entrée anywhere.

Do you know the term *befindlichkeit*? My therapist gave it to me. She often gives me a word, or asks me for one, sometimes an antonym of something I've said, which I find almost magically effective for flipping whatever capsized vessel I might have pulled myself under. This one comes from Heidegger, who, it seems, needed a word for the condition of finding oneself in a situation, a situation that precedes your apprehension of it. Sort of awakening to context. Or even, a sensation of oneself awakening to context. There is no English equivalent, and I guess it is constructed out of the everyday idiomatic question, *Wie befinden Sie sich?*, or literally How do you find yourself, i.e., How are you? *I find myself reeling from my mentor's rebuke*, one might answer.

The four years between the end of my schooling and the

beginning of my teaching career were also the middle years of my ten in New York. They were the years I was in and out of an often maddening, fiercely supportive, loving relationship with Douglas A. Martin, a supremely principled ascetic who was finding traction as an important transgressive novelist. Our reading was a whetstone, and we sharpened on his syllabus: Hervé Guibert, Mohamed Mrabet, Annie Ernaux, Chris Kraus. They were also the years I held these coveted entry positions in literary publishing, where I mimed social graces and wanted to be recognized as worthy of "grooming" but where nearly daily I exhausted myself fighting (gnashing really) countercurrent to the cultural product we were issuing. I was the rare editorial hire at FSG (it helped me to learn and to repeat to others) who wasn't an Ivy League graduate. They were the years my new friends were intrepid adventurers of the city night, who went in every door. I felt I was drawn up and through, like vestibule trash in a draft. At the midpoint of those years one morning the front half of the Q train car I rode to work pulled out of the tunnel onto the Manhattan Bridge, slowly, and paused, and the passengers who could see daylight gasped; moments later when we pulled forward, we all saw the *second* plane strike. We conferred, confided, held silence, cried in bursts, and helped whoever needed to sit, before shooting past all three usual stops to surface at Union Square.

For me, it was a time of continual *befindlichkeit*. It overcame me, I even produced it, as a coping mechanism, I think; it conspired with an expedient passivity I cultivated, made me a character in a story. The *befoundedness* of me, newly alive to an immersive situation, as I'd later relate it, let me touch, but *push* the emotional distress that stacks up when you are underactualized. Is that the word? With my friends, I think we drank so much to invite the come-what-may situations in which we would find, even *catch* ourselves. We often started the night at a place aptly named Anyway Café.

I found myself mugged by a man at gunpoint who had followed me to my building's front door. He said not to turn around, he'd just gotten out of prison, needed my money, and didn't want to do this the hard way. He reached around and into my front jeans pocket. I found myself sitting down to lunch with Jonathan Galassi, who wanted to ask me about edgy new poets. I remember he ordered a kir royale, but I don't remember if I asked what that was. I found myself holding still in a squeaky seat next to my friend Jason in the third row at The Gaiety between acts. Which meant, he said, now the strippers would come back out without their jockstraps. They're getting fluffed. After, I walked him back to work. I found myself in a muddled ecstasy craving more abuse to befall Douglas's shiftless protagonists in the manuscripts he gave me to read. I knew it was a kind of genius. Nothing I'd read had ever embroiled me as much as the abject creeping around harm he cultivated from his diary notebooks. He had saved his life as a writer, risked it again in memory, and abetted the brutalization of the innocent he was who knew better. It was dark, late. I had heard train service was running again to Brooklyn. I found myself walking down the middle of Park Avenue South, suddenly surrounded, flanked, left and right by silent rows of armed National Guardsmen streaming out of the Armory in formation, walking at my pace.

To answer *How do you find yourself?* by providing a quick-take account of the more prepossessing recent circumstances of your life is to forgo, to rush past, affective knowledge. How did it feel?

The last few years when I have taught narrative, I've used an exercise to develop character out of sentience first. I've come to call it Out of the Pocket. I guess it comes from my amateur training in movement improv and maybe, too, the practice of keeping a dream journal. Usually it follows the class's study of Samuel Beckett's *Molloy*. I think about Molloy's style of *befindlichkeit*, radically oblivious but inferring with each step what seems to be the case for him and the immediate world he's in, some kind of forest he traverses for reasons he faintly understands. Early on, after an incident on a hill, he descends "to retrieve my bicycle," he says, "(I didn't know I had one)." And, before the famous sucking stones passage, Molloy is surprised to recall, reaching in his pocket, that he has collected pebbles for this diversion. Before we prepare to write, I suggest we demonstrate the technique I have in mind in an interview format. I volunteer myself first, we're seated in a circle, and I describe my loose intention to speak as a character with no attributes yet. I ask that everyone close their eyes. I close mine. I begin with sensations and proprioception— cool or warm, tired or alert, standing or lying down, indoors or out, alone or not—gradually broadening out concentrically from the character's body and station to what he sees and hears and so forth. As the teller, I am invited to follow a description or declaration (I'm walking in the gravel in my dress shoes, playing a kind of game with my balance) with a speculation (It must be Sunday; no one is paying any mind). I will have told the students that as auditors they may ask questions to motivate the story: *What's that sound?* (I don't know; traffic?) *Is there anything in your jacket pocket?* (Yes, a carefully torn square of paper with writing on it.) The story developed this way is almost always backstory. Experience gathers behind the character who at first seems so new to life. In their dark—or maybe they've opened their eyes—the students lead. *What does the paper say?* (It's an address, a return address.)

On the Understory

Permitting Shame, Error and Guilt, Myself the Single Source

The understory is the second, subsidiary layer of growth in a forest, the fern and moss layer, the groundcover and shrubs that necessarily proliferate early and late in the season when the canopy overhead is patchiest and light can break through. Saplings from parent trees grow to a point in the understory, but ultimately it's not their realm. It's the world, rather, of small shade-tolerant trees and hard berry bushes, currants, holly; of rhododendron in squat enclaves; and, deepest in, perhaps a surprise lily or orchid, suggesting maturity of ecosystem. Dogwood is a very early bloomer, mid-March, showing itself thereby as an understory tree even when planted alone and central in front-yard redbrick North Carolina or Virginia, where, as in several southern states, it is the state tree. A white-blossom branch of it extends beneath a perched cardinal on license plates. One wishes them back in the woods.

The understory so defined, so described overhead, is a theater of sorts, and of course the word seems narratological. My novelist friend Samantha once reminded me walking in the forest near Woodstock, New York, where fog collects in the hollows and routinely some kind of chittering cannot be identified, that this is the faerie realm of leprechaun and hobbit, of elfin activity generally. Samantha is a dark, imaginative writer of Irish extraction and some of her stories sneak up on the real or legendary, legendarily lonely, figures who wander the wilderness behind the MetroNorth villages of Sleepy Hollow or Mount Kisco in Westchester and Duchess Counties. A man who walked a circuit around the Catskills for thirty years after the shock of the death of his wife was one. The genus loci possessing the woodlands in the British Isles rose again from damp similarity in the fresh rot of deciduous New England.

In the South, where I'm from—where, once, off the Blue Ridge Parkway I demonstrated for Samantha you can work your arm elbow deep down in the loam under the overhang of old rhododendron—the derivation is less direct, more perverse. I think of the Disney animated version of *Robin Hood* that I grew up with, which had an accompanying children's record and storybook I believe. In it, Sherwood Forest is still Sherwood Forest, and the voice of Robin Hood, animated as a fox in a feathered green toque and trim green vestments, is debonair, intelligent, quite British, and might well be Peter Sellers; but the narration from the very opening scenes is delivered by a down-home heavyset-sounding country raconteur: a Tom T. Hall, but more molasses. The narrator rather soon in the movie breaks into song as we watch the two friends travel a trail: *Robin Hood and Little John were walkin' through the fowrest / each one a gigglin' at whut the other'n had to say.* The camaraderie is sylvan, a little magical, but in the mix of heritage the voice suggests whose woods these are: light-dappled, Appalachian. The episteme is lyric nostalgia: for shirtless, carefree white American summer boyhood south of the Mason-Dixon. Outlaw wandering into woods, fraternity under the radar. This adaptation, and its narrative voiceover, must have been a model for *The Dukes of Hazzard*, the early Eighties TV series whose heroes' guerilla social services and efforts at rural redistribution of resources were at odds with *their* county's sheriff and magistrate. "Lost sheep to shepherd" was the call on the CB by one of the Duke boys, either one, to Uncle Jesse back home. It was pastoral. Their nature was unreconstructed.

What between cousins was granted concealment that would have been criminal out in the open; how free was "just a little bit more than the law will allow," as the show's theme song confessed? Atavism is built into—and the active agent in—the *good ole boy*;

it's the element that signals mischief (he's just a *good boy* without it). A vestigial order outside present law, an *old* South, is evidently his lost Arcadia. Everyone on hand is there to tend and protect his errant revenant ways (Bo Peep is cousin Daisy's handle), or drive the lost sheep home. Iconography of the white supremacist order is confined to the Duke boys' vehicle, the *General Lee*; its horn plays the first bar of Dixie, the confederate flag is emblazoned on its roof, its blue-belted X visible only by aerial vantage. The macro message is clear. But each time the plot involves Bo and Luke's evasion of the law, their vindication of a way of life upholds not sullen, menacing Jim Crow injustice but, rather, the family's distillation and distribution of moonshine. Uncle Jesse has a still somewhere on the farm. (Seems like a cover.) To protect the family business from law enforcement and the community from corrupt meddlers was why these good ole boys "straighten the curves" on the back roads, which they know best. Each episode, in short, one is asked to overlook a certain amount of unease or opaqueness to support a campaign of tried-and-true, on-the-ground familiarity over synoptic, monitory knowledge.

The tangle of back roads through Patrick Springs and Horse Pasture and Bassett and Critz, in Patrick and Henry Counties in southwestern Virginia, are ones my father and uncles and aunt know well. My grandparents Walter and Irene lived right on Route 58, the state's longest east-west thoroughfare, wending from Virginia Beach all the way to the Kentucky line. Their small brick home was on a stretch of open road between Martinsville and Galax. For me it had diametric energies. At the rear of it, the cinderblock basement opened onto a (most years) fallow plot and a gravelly clay lane down into the forest. And, from the small front window, at her seat at the flecked Formica kitchen table, my grandmother watched the traffic roar past or else pull in to poke around the perpetual yard sale. Most of her children grew up to be highwaymen of one sort or another, including my father,

Curtis, who left home for truck driving school in Winston as soon as he finished high school. In their sixties, he and my aunt Janice each still ride their Harleys down to Key West and out to Sturgis. I should not have been surprised that, the night before Grandma's funeral last winter, the visitation line was full of family friends paying respects in their best black leather jackets. My uncle Paul, before his early death from diabetes and alcoholism, was her roughest, most worrisome child, in and out of trouble with police and probation officers, and certainly the most recognizable on the road. He drove a boxy, bug-eyed brown 1960s Ford Econoline van, on whose side he had painted the words *Lil Brown Jug.* Three lethal X's on the jug itself.

It wasn't until her final sickness that I got from my father stories about how Grandma as a young girl had been assigned the job of lookout in her family. Halfway down the hillside was her daily post. Her role was crucial: to run up to the hilltop house and report what kind of vehicle was winding up the road to pay a visit, patrol car or customer. The still and its works were prepared or vanished accordingly. She had been private, ashamed maybe, about the facts of her childhood. But it gave a context for her later habits, her constant occupations, at that table at which I sat with her long hours as a little boy, while wrestling or *Dukes of Hazzard* blared in the living room where the men cussed and snored at turns. On the table were her three mainstays: the CB radio, the police scanner, and her ashtray. (On Sundays a fourth: a transistor, for Preacher Corns's sermon from Spoon Creek.) We would listen to the static feed of trucker communication in and among state troopers on duty. I could dial for a frequency that was active: good buddies establishing location, relaying positions. Lots were men whose families she knew. We understood each other; we were both quiet, observant, even furtively vigilant, clever. In our games (endless dominoes, cards, fly-swatting) she let her rascally manner emerge; it was also in her asides and maneuvers, holding her own and staying above the fray, in the company of men. We were attuned. We made good scanners.

It was in this particular legacy and landscape and their concealments that my imaginative life developed. The *fort-da* dynamic was most determinative here. Without fail I could always return to this person who seemed to see me clearly, and occupy with her the seated center of all the transit and crosstalk she had surrounding her, and meantime set out age eight, nine, ten, into the woods out back to explore, unwatched, unguided. Often alone, or sometimes with my younger cousin Tammy following me, I made shallow expeditions, prowling the leafy territory with a long stick until "stations" suggested themselves, according entirely to the propitious qualities of certain areas in the understory. A mound surrounded by fallen pinecones and a nearby small clearing might suggest a factory floor, a labor to oversee, a procedure. We would set to work. Tammy and I neatened our barracks at a moss bed or made distress calls from a phone booth (tree trunk) or leapt into position in a small earthen recess I recall fitting us like bucket seats. We'd sound the horn that sounded like getaway, and holler the yell. Or, we agreed where Kmart and the pool hall and the hospital were and made our rounds, reporting to each other in a stream of pretend what office of adulthood we were managing under what duress and what next, intermittently cresting in present, phenomenal reality when we found a black widow or a terrapin or a shotgun shell to study.

A similar energy obtained to the years-long indoor practice I was developing about this time, in privacy, actually with—as I recall it now—almost abject secrecy. I made maps. Each map I made invented a place, a place suggested by the schematic of the place, as beheld from an implicit aerial vantage. There was a procedure. A kind of early experiment with determinism. With my hands on the white knobs of an Etch A Sketch, and with eyes closed, I would dial in a line drawing of what would be, when

I had finished and could review, a region or countryside, with creeks and borders—or a town with roads diverging immoderately from north-south or east-west axes, suggesting landscape. Surveying, one could assess where the area's prominent intersections were, and one could imagine where families lived, where schools or theaters or ponds or prisons were. One could even—before Google Maps—transmit oneself down to ground level to imagine tableaux from certain spots. I would fastidiously and laboriously copy the map over to larger dimensions on paper, on a plat of many sheets of 8½ by 11 notebook paper taped together. I suppose I knew then what I found articulated much later (by cartographic theorist James Corner): any image can be a map and any map can be a gameboard. To wit, it was my job, furthermore, to create sets of outcomes according to dice rolls—and limited to my narrow estimation of the range of possible human doing. All of this was preparation for play. By the time I rolled to determine the daily "turn" of each "player," I had mostly exhausted the fun of the game. It was about the *activation* of potentialities. Another key feature of these maps was that they could be folded quickly and put away if I heard anyone approach. What is it I would have been caught doing had I been discovered in this reverie by, for instance, my mother's new boyfriend Jeff? Corner would answer, by extension of Donald Winnicott's theories about spatialized play: I was supplementing a self, building a selfhood. These maps were integral to me. As I write this, longhand, in seat 21E on a flight from Tucson to New York, my urge is to cover it as I would a poem, with the shell of my left hand, to shield it from the passenger in 21D. Meanwhile, 21F looks out the window onto the colorful rectilinear floorplan beneath us.

The first map I can remember seeing was a large, minutely detailed road map of the United States, on the wood-paneled wall of my father's largely metal office at the corner of a freight warehouse lined with loading bays. Cracked, compacted black rubber at the lip of each. In Charlotte, he was, for a time, while we were all still together, a tractor trailer dispatch manager. The long-haulers reported in to him from routes all over the country. It was partly his job, as I recall or as I imagined then, to update their positions frequently, all day long. He preferred driving. I'm sure my map play was a way to attain perspective on, and manage, my father's absence after he left. I could oversee and play out the courses any number of lives were charting simultaneously, mine and his but two of them. He had given me, Christmas after Christmas, several toy semi trucks; but any page of an atlas was more alive for me. A map is a depot of futurities, a staging ground, a theater of operations, James Corner says, its performative power comes from its being both analogous—indexical—and compositional.

As you drive east to west across this continent, past the Mississippi, past the Missouri River, there is a certain point by which the interstate roadkill has changed, where flattened gray squirrel corpses have given way to the spilled piggish innards of armadillos, bright red butcheries, each one. It means that the constant tree canopy of the eastern seaboard has subsided, there is more sky overhead, and one's line of vision is here and there unbroken by anything at all. The thinning begins perhaps in western Indiana, and by central Oklahoma, except in rare riparian areas, there is mostly open sky. The terrain more closely resembles the map of it. Here one may project, as mapmakers long did, a prospect, from which the overview too is unimpeded.

★ ★ ★

For eight of the last nine years I have lived in the West. It is a fact of life that we are exposed here, exposed by the sun, exposed to one another. There is no understory, because there is no leafy shade in southern Arizona. Everything that grows is ground-cover, but coverage is spotty; the pervasive scatter of rubble is the degree zero look of planetary entropy. Nothing about the landscape is opaque or concealing. If the presence of something animal is undisclosed, it is due to its alert stillness, or its celerity out ahead of you, or its subterranean or nocturnal life. My own pet theory is that human morality, competitiveness, and prurient interest in one's neighbor are reduced here, not encouraged or conditioned by tree cover and mutual obscurity, as in New England. Puritanism didn't make it this far, or not without significant reform. And without an atmosphere of cover, pretenses for rearguard behavior do not thrive, as in the South. In the Sonoran desert, one knows well all four kinds of tree that grow without special irrigation: mesquite, ironwood, acacia, palo verde. The latter two are sometimes referred to as bushes. Where biodiversity is relatively limited, one knows what one is looking at, makes note of when and where, in which saguaro knothole, the Gila woodpecker is nesting. He becomes a student of how a gradual climb of fifty feet across a half mile brings at that altitude an entirely new subspecies of agave or peculiar single-stitch knitted grasses or signs of pack rats amid the thatch of dropped fingerlings under teddy bear cholla. Baby quail arrival means it's April, and it will be early summer when the little ones have sprouted the clumsy curlicue plumes on their heads long enough to bob. Today John and I looked out on the circus of our backyard, where a young twitchy bunny was querying each fellow resident: the quail chicks in their family retinue, the standing ground squirrels sunning front feet up, the stone-pumping lizard, and the leggy roadrunner. Beat it, bunny.

Where I grew up, under the pine and hickory and maple of the central piedmont, I spent my private, creative life enacting a wish to rise up and out, to see the thing in full, attain a supervisory perspective. My familiarity down below with surface conditions, on the ground, was only ever great enough to keep myself safe, to stave off danger assiduously, to forgo and aver and beg off situationally, and I never found how to blend in or belong, not without covering who I was, which was exhausting. So, to keep part of myself outside and beyond the realm of my family and peers was a service to my authentic self, wherever he was. The prospect I projected (and projected from) was more or less the vantage of advisement, a guardian angel's eye view. Consider the prospect poem, at its height in the eighteenth century; it was set here, at more or less standard Romantic counseling distance, Wordsworth high above Tintern Abbey (sister Dorothy gets an earful of perspective), or Thomas Gray above Eton College. And perhaps more to the point, so were many early queer autobiographical novels, often in an omniscient, reparative second person point of view, self-supervising, for instance, Christopher Isherwood's *Down There On a Visit*, which lowers into Christopher's life at various junctures, looking in on the pilgrim's progress. Shuttling from present vantage, after the heretofore. Which is the method, too, of C. S. Giscombe's *Here*, my favorite book of poetry, the one I get the most inside. I come to feel and trust the appeal to what he calls "the long view," a kind of practice of surveying at large the "outlying areas" in the urban South, the unincorporated areas, "distributorships," "service track," where race is *in* the land. There is a point in the book where in the span of like ten words he tries on the Look Away of Dixie and the Dear Sister of Wordsworth, throwing shade and taking umbrage, both.

But since I have lived in the West, in Missoula and now in Tucson, two valley cities where total overview is imminently attainable, indeed where arguably (in the case of the Bitterroot Valley, where Missoula is the county seat) the positional sense of an "us down here" characterizes the living there, beneath the mountains alongside, I am becoming the other kind of knower, the empiricist, aground and terrestrial and canvassing about. Merrill Gilfillan, a poet of the Western high plains who has a genius for this above-below shuttling, calls the shift in attention,

PROXIES

this tightening of referents, moving "from the realm of *savoir* to the realm of *connaître*." Perhaps it is because now I know I *can* climb out that I am also content to be in the weeds.

There is a point precisely at the ridgeline of Water Works Hill, north end of Missoula, in the high cinquefoil grasses that dry out midsummer and give the Bitterroot its bright hue, where the grasshopper behavior changes. I mean, presumably, one subspecies gives way to another. My guess is they're territorial. Walking on the south face of the mountain, you find that at about one stride's distance the grasshoppers leap away from you, forward or to either side, hip high, an insect fountain effect, sedulously avoiding contact with you; whereas, in the small canted plateau at the top and on the north and northwest face they leap blindly as you approach, springing chaotically into your body as often as away from it. When I made this discovery it was sonic, musical, before it was conscious; the metal water bottle I carry was all of a sudden pinging, like a Brian Eno composition, and I had walked twenty feet before I understood what was happening.

I felt like Gilbert White of Selborne and wished to start a letter with this finding, a "letter to the same," as each new entry is titled in my edition of his 1770s issuances about the minutiae of the natural world in the village where he was pastor. In any one dispatch he might modify with a new observation an earlier years-old assertion about the habits of martins around the barn in autumn, or correlate the darkness of alluvial mud to the health of tortoise hatchlings, or speculate on the nature of congenital mental illness, or detail how it seems a goldfish prepares to die. In my edition there are no letters in return, but the preface says he's sending to someone in a county north, a sort of botanist I think. He's a pastor, a protestant, and so of course all the data are for him evidence of divine reach; but he doesn't seem interested in synoptic conclusions. His trade is in neighborly empiricism.

I have an old early hazy memory of sitting with Grandma on her back step, each of us with a fly swatter, concentrating on the busy industry of the inky black ants at our feet, on the little square of cement jutting into the grass. Just watching, remarking their little fellowships, wanding over one another with antennae, then moving down the line. Maybe it wasn't that same day but I remember my father had yelled at her and slammed the storm door, and I was too scared to join him; I knew the way he tore up those roads when he was angry, so I stayed behind with Grandma. Eventually my mother remarried; I grew up, moved far away, became so different, and we were so seldom in touch I felt guilty for the relative impunity I had in that family, as her favorite. We connected again in her last years, and a few days before she died she left me a harrowing rhapsodic message, from the hospital, a minute or so long (I still have it) in which she simply repeats my name, the way she said it, in one long syllable, a dozen waves of the live word and sometimes "O!" in between. When she died, I lost membership in an "us down here." My oldest one, the surest, my first, one I never had to conform or fabricate to fit. I never saw *her* go off into those woods we were facing. But she must have; she knew what I meant when I told her about how, when you lie in the leaves looking up, the whole mood could change if the wind blows the tall trees together and apart.

On the Near Term

Permitting Shame, Error and Guilt, Myself the Single Source

About a year and a half ago, I was walking on the campus of UC Boulder, where I was presenting at AndNow, the conference of experimental literature (one of the first places I read one of these essays, the one on housesitting, on a panel called The Queer Heart), and I raced to catch up with my old friend Frances Richard and the writer Kevin Killian (who would also be on the panel). They were walking together in a quad and turned, seemed glad to see me. After hugs and hellos, Frances added, "Where do you *even live* now?" No doubt I read into her emphasis, but it was a sinking feeling to manage a sanguine response in front of Kevin, whom I had long admired. It had been nine years since my first book and would be another six months before my second, I was not on Facebook or anyplace to follow or tag, I had bounced between temporary teaching gigs, bottoming out a bit in Boston, before moving to Tucson without certain prospect. I think I answered (the insinuation I was dead?) that in the near term, while my partner John—whom Kevin knew—was going back to school for an MSW, I was teaching what classes I could get at the U of A, and helping sort affairs after my stepfather's death, trying to relish the underemployment for the time it gave me to finish a book of essays. "The near term" has been part of my answer to inquiries about my career for a while now. In fact I just this week lost my appointment, such as it was, at the university's Honors College, which is confusing in a year when I have had some, you know, real recognition as a writer, and success in the classroom. My severance came in the second paragraph of a reply to a gratifying note I had forwarded the dean from a student effusive about our semester. After exclaiming how great the note was (she is remarkably expert at exclaiming in otherwise obdurate email), she reported that my next class was being given to one of her full-time faculty and they had agreed to move away from adjunct contracts. She hoped we'd cross paths again. So: In the near term, I'm lucky to have a grant from the Howard Foundation (a year's salary, in Tucson dollars), I'm riding my bike in the rubble and doing my little radio show, and we're looking for a way to stay in this city we love and love each other in, and meantime casting about for teaching job security elsewhere.

"The near term" is an expression whereby the open indefinite future is parceled so as to be more manageable. As the most immediate of the stages it implies—the one starting now—it is invoked especially when such management in planning is paramount; its definition is relative to a later span, the distant future or some mid-range period, for instance. It has an outer parameter, one that is not, like that of *the meantime*, contingent upon the onset of an anticipated event; its expiration is more loosely understood. The near term is a good example of the way in which time is routinely comprehended by spatial analogy: already in this paragraph to discuss how it means what it means, the parlance has availed five such metaphors: stage, span, distant, range, and outer. *Near term*, it seems to me, increasingly surpasses *short term* in prevalence, relegating the latter to adjectival use only. It brings the next while closer, into the subject's domain. There is the soft suggestion that the near term *belongs to* the subject—as a sediment apron belongs to a volcanic event, after. To an extent.

Moreover the near term has a deictic function. The duration in question is brought into the kin of hither-markers, words like *this* or *these* or *here* or *now*, opposite the set of terms by definition outside such orbit: *that, those, there, yonder, then*. It is thus absorbed into a contradistinction. The division is unbreachable, but gauging where the liminal membrane is (where here starts and there begins) is the inexact and constant business of the relational dialectic inherent in language. Wherever it is set, its rule is firm: grammatically, you cannot "come there," for instance, just as you cannot "go here." (My birth name, Overby, was likely a deictic, away in the mind's eye.) Deictics indicate the relative station of the speaker, and in certain languages with ingenious grammars, they are built right into words as suffixes and prefixes. In Spanish I think "come down here to me" can be said in one word. In German *hierankommen* might do similar work. As a new learner of Chinese twenty years ago it was remarkable to me how much conversation with native Mandarin speakers is filled with *zhei ge* and *nei ge*, (this and that), which are said, like *um* or *y'know*, while casting for the proper word, giving meanwhile the preliminary information as to whether the still unforthcoming referent is in the inner or outer zone, peripersonal or beyond. These green beans. That star.

There is, incidentally, a curious exception to this side/that side deictic absolutes and proprietary binaries, one with which some gay and bisexual men are familiar. In clips of English-language (here I pause to wonder whether the same is true in Chinese) video pornography that I date to the last eight years or so, you occasionally hear one sex partner say to the other, in a kind of unique ventriloquy, referring to his own anatomy, "take that dick," or, alternatively, "do you like that ass?" *That* and *those* taking up residence squarely in this-territory; it seems to me an act just shy of identifying by the third-person pronoun. I could be wrong, but I don't think this sort of self-othering speech is an attribute of straight porn, at least not bidirectionally. (Nor have I experienced it exactly in live sex, certainly not in sex with only one partner.) And, to be honest, when I encounter it there is often a particular accompanying effect that doesn't excite me or that shuts off a valve of open interest. It can seem to me too closely related to group sexual assault, the signification of which is not arousing to me, and the real act of which (from hazing to rape) is unequivocally hideous. In the traffic of phrases are ones that an onlooking accomplice to violence might hurl to pump the mortification of the victim. And in other instances, it means riding an ethical precipice, to overhear and continue to listen to what may (or may not) be someone's post-traumatic self-distancing reaction formation. I'd like to say any whiff of that is a direct biological shutdown for me. I'm not sure. But when it is stimulative, when it's hot, this reverse deictic, it is usually because in the one partner's express projection into the other's subject position there is a taste for his pleasure, consulting his pleasure. It is, additionally, part of what makes the speaker's possible sexual versatility legible; some men know what *that* feels like. I suppose it is an extension of an experience everyone can identify with; if you are giving someone a massage (erotic or not), are you likelier to ask *How does this feel* or *How does that feel?* What is the difference? There a subtle shift in agency, in empathy. Isn't there?

Once in Boston, on the subway, riding with John, I saw the star of my sometime fantasy life. His name, though I am sure it was not his name, was Billy. The name belonged to his boyish looks; in his early twenties probably, he had retained an actual flush in his cheeks, which along with black curly hair, a compact frame, lean but not slender, and an idiosyncratic fleshy twist of a mouth, gave him an unpracticed allure. Big eyes, slow blink, a farmer's thumbnails—good wide square windows, double dimple at the small of his back. Even now I could draw a pretty good likeness of the contour of his instep. Not that I could take much of any of that in when, sitting across from him, I first recognized him. He was already looking at me, and I wonder if my whole body jerked to the realization I made; in any case, I betrayed enough of a tell that he read right away I had seen the videos, all four or five I knew about in fact, in which he has sex with two older men, probably thirty-five and fifty. The men were themselves a couple, at least in the premise of their video channel. Their specialty was amateur "nonfiction" video in which they reveal how they meet each of their successive partners, almost always younger—from the bar or over the internet as a result of their huge following and probably ad revenue. Billy was a recurring participant. One clip was in fact called "The Return of Billy." It may be the one in which they go to a campground and fuck in a cabin. The men apparently trade the camera and Billy is told about his body, directed by lewd nudges, and interviewed aggressively about the body nearest him. He rolls his eyes at one point, in all the revving libido and corny talk. *This*, he seems to think, is too much.

When John looked up from his book, Billy looked away, but wore a lingering grin when I next glanced. I felt spotted, read, known in my situation—as the older half of a couple who keeps his autoerotic life separate from his partner and, furthermore, a clearly ardent viewer of the situational precarity of men his type. Or do I mean, men my type? If I really examine the embarrassment it felt like being apprehended in a regressive state, the one endemic to the routine consumption of porn in its present plenitude, the state in which the inviolability of one's near-deictic is guaranteed. A shame. One's relationship to the mediated images of sex is structurally infantile (his only options are disappointment and interest), and lost is the opportunity (largely foreclosed by screen-viewing) to project oneself anywhere *there* or *then* in fantasy. Billy was laughing a little to himself as the ride went on, and I recall the train that day made me slide around laterally on the plastic bench, repeatedly sort of crashing into John before coasting away again. I had to square myself and grip. The condition seemed peculiarly mine alone. Billy-watched. It was Boston, so Billy may well have been a student; it's not a great stretch to project in a blink Laura Mulvey in the pursed-open knapsack at his feet.

John's type is perhaps the same as Billy's. He and I acknowledge, and enjoy acknowledging, that he is drawn to a couple categories of men—the Sears model American dad kind of guy and (they overlap only in their optimal dimness and disinterest) the jock, especially a certain dirty, surly variety, with the sort of upper body you could kind of climb if he let you. That I am neither of those is, I want to say, incidental. We are a couple, and as such who knows how unusual. We have a practice of pointing out the relative physical merits and the attentions (or even the stray glances) of men in our midst; John attracts more attention than I do, more beautiful now than when we met even, and more confidently and whimsically stylish. We have a term for the looks one or both of us collects in public: *pageviews.* Just the other night my page got viewed. Even as John was standing in a charming ceremony at the hard-carpeted fore of the Ward 6 Tucson City Council office receiving a PFLAG scholarship for the final year of his master's program, the young punk friend of another recipient in the front row stole a couple of glances back at me, tested me for reciprocation. Looked again during the cobbler and punch reception. Later John says, "Oh, him. He was too waifish for you."

We maintain a running patter of men on the side like pleasure is our business, the business of our partnership; the Billy ride, for instance, has become part of institutional memory. John tells the story better than I do now. And I tease him about his old co-worker Dana, the bad-seed hottie who rode a crotch rocket to work, and had built an effective gruff mystique around his sexiness. John fell mute once introducing us, he was so undone. They got off at the same time and, when we had only the one car to share and I would pick John up from work, it was often comically awkward. Dana, helmeted, would straddle his bike and strap in but always let us pull out of the lot first. A routine organized by the hurry of John's agony, on which we could obliquely remark after we turned into traffic. I guess I mean, we have not excluded the appeal of men everywhere from our shared love life. Nor from our union a subscription to the artful ingenuity of queer semiotics—tells, covers, reveals, small-town code. It's part of the adventure, we seem to have decided, together to look out and see who's looking in. We find something to trust in how we keep upping our respective permissive appetites for each other's independence as a desire-marked body in the world. There is injury in it, so we keep feeling where the good risk is.

With each other physically we are like a couple of elk, or something rarer and even more complexly antlered; there are whole seasons when in our need we get kind of stuck in the lock of our racks and settle for nuzzling. And then, occasionally, a breakthrough, and it can feel like molting might feel, velvety after, and then the good itch for new growth. Easy, confident, lissome, open; *we should do this all the time.* A near term begins.

Was it in coffee spoons that Eliot's aging Prufrock lamented he had measured time, and was it incontinence he worried over in the "dare I eat a peach" aside? It's quite legible, too, as an anal-receptive concern. Modernity has developed an anxious consciousness of male sexual performance (among other consciousnesses of performances) and its relationship to time. The interval between orgasms can fully preoccupy men (and couples), and more than we want to acknowledge, plans by the millions right now are being measured out from points of recentmost detumescence. How soon is now? Wouldn't Tuesday be better? Don't fool yourself: if John Boehner hasn't in the fussy sortilege of male self-regulation optimized his supposed potency for the next important vote on the floor, or even retrofitted the docket, he would be an exception. It has always seemed to me that a queerness worthy of the word would at the least own and, better, undermine the ticking hegemony of such time-keeping.

I have lived in the near term this whole time. In and out of twenty years of relationships with men. Holding in reserve some of the self committed to another. A dynamic in which, writ large, one or both of us gradually understood that there would be, after us, life again for each of us, and accorded accordingly. (I was late to both/and thinking.) Being alone had seemed to me—my own regrettable limitation—to be off the clock.

Daily life with John in a thousand ways retools my experience of time and term and togetherness. He has a certain enduring fantasy he calls *self storage*, and in it we operate such a facility, with front offices for writing and making and maybe answering the phone. Everyone loading up cells in rows along the linear hive we head up. But like most of John's designs it has a metaphysics activated by merely conceptualizing it. I mean, self storage is somehow already our game, bidirectionally, the business of our partnership. Once we decided to start a venture of uncertain cultural production, a magazine in one iteration, called You Be Tonya. I went to the hardware store in Jamaica Plain and had a faux-wood office-door nameplate engraved. YBT gets mail, from a Japanese paper store in San Francisco, from Friends of the Rookery in Cleveland. It's still what we call our thing. You Be Tonya produced a study of masculinity once, in which was diagrammed for Missoula a local flowchart of *mascules* (units of masculinity, we determined, that transfer person to person in any social transaction).

The house we rent is very nearly in the open desert west of town because that's where we can afford a three-bedroom home in which two rooms can be offices. In John's right now I am permitted the following inventory: on the cranked high drafting table among many items, atop a bright ceramic lettuce leaf, a mourning dove nest he found yesterday in which is depressed a fresh ovoid memory. Above it, an Oberlin alumni wall calendar whose first two rows of days are obscured with brown packing paper across which is written in red, mysteriously, "next Saturday." Wedged high in the corner an ever-changing mobile of cut paper and bent wire. Gone are the palm fronds but draped along the bottom arc of a suspended embroidery hoop is a small sprig of serviceberry. On the floor a large sketchbook open to a new page with a figure part man part gallows drying in streaky purple marker (no, it's an outline of Pfaueninsel, the peacock island with the fraught history we visited last summer in Germany) beside a small notebook on which, among other marvels, is written "capitalism with the cowlick in his hair" and the definition of a word, *kneippism*, which (both word and definition) might be invented: "a form of hydrotherapy that involves walking barefoot through morning dew." A number of artworks are tacked on the other walls, including John's own sensational charcoal female nudes and layered paper silhouettes among monograph prints: a portrait of a bearded, Civil War convalescent in long underwear and a hand-tinted nude male torso surrendering to the viewer Saint Sebastian–style. *Tender Buttons* is crammed with paper, alongside the self-healing X-acto board. Two white string ladders of varying length are laid across a notions box, two of four found on separate days in the street, like the fragments of spider webs Gilbert White chronicled raining over Selbourne and vicinity, never explained, one afternoon in the 1750s.

John's intuition as a writer is quicksilver, and his creativity is completely disinhibited, high metabolism. The act of prismatic writing Roland Barthes called intransitive. His projects are procedural (sometimes stages two and three will follow stage one years later), and have a delicious way of sneaking up on subjectivity. My favorite thing in life is a day of immersive writing sessions, my cell by his, nuns in our squints, studio backchanneling here and there to share. It would not be uncommon on such a day to find John writing *through*, say, Wittgenstein's *Remarks on Color* and a Barbara Pym novel, or Michelle Tea's hustler journals and William Maxwell's *The Folded Leaf.* That kind of companioned reading is generative for his particular project of (unfastened) annotative writing. An integrative intelligence tracking, offroading. Plus, on his large desktop screen like a clock a two-and-a-half-hour men's field hockey match from 2006, Sri Lanka v. The Netherlands, might be unspooling (starting with the camera's rousingly close man-by-man pan of the teams lined up for anthem singing), and on his laptop a playlist of successive unboxing videos: ardent young sensualists worldwide reviewing Yankee Candle purchases. *Clean Towels. Autumn Spice.* He stops writing in his notebook temporarily to text our friend Jason an outré suggestion about his Bad Kids film studies syllabus. He is following all this. It is a project of following, leading the symphony.

It's a pleasure to catalog the curatorial maximalism that is John at work, to lose my way in it even. Where was I? Time is reorganized in it, as it is in Gertrude Stein. His notebooks, which he started eleven years ago, at a time he recognizes as a rebirth, number well into the hundreds. There have been dozens since we met. They are numbered; every inch on both sides of each page is full. His current work is to read them one at a time, achronologically, culling phrases and formulations, assembling something new, calibrating to the present. He sometimes recovers a poem almost entirely intact. From notebook 72 he types up such a poem today, "I Hire an Aunt," which is a part of a series of other "I Hire" poems, supple, incremental, loving, which may address the crisis of agency and strategy of adaptation from the perspective of the partner of a perennial finalist for professorships. They remind me of an earlier sequence of his, "Desirable in a Shipmate." He shows me another page, still in his raw script, from the night we stayed in Gloucester, where I gave a reading before the stage converted to a platform bed after the patrons left and the mattress came out. The evening's atmosphere is recorded. There is my nosebleed from three and a half years ago, and here is Gerrit Lansing poking me with the end of his cane to get my attention: best flirt ever. A pretty boy in his twenties, tattoos and tiny Toms, comes in to the two-story coffee shop where John and I are writing this morning. Very Tucson. He is carrying a very young, sleepy Cocker Spaniel, beautifully brushed. We watch from the loft alcove we have made our perch. A text from across the table arrives. "The puppy is redundant." It all sews together.

Our first date was on Election Day, 2010. Or, it's truer to say, we were dating by the end of that day, a day on which we had set out early from Missoula across the Lolo pass into Idaho, where we hiked six miles into the woods; John knew about a series of stepped natural hot springs. It was an eventful hike— newts and pheasants and dizzy spells and falls into the creek. We walked out after dusk—dark enough we needed the car's head- lights to change into dry socks. We kissed in the beams, which made the little globes on the ghostberry bush galactic. We mark our anniversary out from there, and we tell everyone every year we re-elect each other. *Campaign* comes from the Latin *campus*. Open country. And *country* from *contra*. All the area out in front of you, facing you. No term limits. The queer heart.

For now, I ride my little bike out into the rubble. Sun over- head. I carry poetry to the radio station. We write our books. We pay the dollar, swim at Himmel Pool. We even live here.

Correction.

The Little Professor calculator game, released by Texas Instruments in 1976, featured on its packaging a squat-faced cartoon professor, in glasses and mustaches, and while he had a certain avian character, he was meant to be human and not owl.

"The Owl in the Sarcophagus" is largely about pathetic fallacy, specifically the human tendency to reconfigure and repurpose the sounds of nature for particular commemorations or grief. The speaker hears himself hear "good-by" in the heights of the forest, "because the ear repeats, / Without a voice, inventions of farewell."

The word *owl* appears in five other poems by Wallace Stevens, including "Someone Puts a Pineapple Together," where it takes its turn in a list of twelve apposite metaphors for the fruit positioned for a still life: "An owl sits humped. It has a hundred eyes."

Aaron Kunin is writing a book about character as form. Imagine a lounge where characters develop before (re)entering the field of literature.

Dallas Green was the manager of the Philadelphia Phillies in 1981. His career managerial record was 454–478, a winning percentage of .487.

Brothers of the Head, the mockumentary by filmmakers Lou Pepe and Keith Fulton, like the eponymous science fiction novel by Brian Aldiss from which it is adapted, is set in the early 1970s.

In the film, the conjoined twins are in a band called Bang Bang. Neither is gay-identified.

The alternate ending of Depeche Mode's "Somebody"—"And in a place like this I'll get away with it"—was added to the band's 1988 performance at the Pasadena Rose Bowl, where the live album *101* was recorded. The song as written and first recorded on the studio album *Some Great Reward* concludes, "But in a case like this I'll get away with it."

It is likely that the Br'er Rabbit stories were Muscogee or Creek Indian in origin. Cherokee tradesmen enslaved the Muscogee during their frequent, sweeping seventeenth-century raids of other Native peoples in Georgia, Florida, and the Carolinas. In subsequent generations, these slaves were conjoined and kept with African slaves in colonial plantation servitude, resulting in a mixture of heritage.

In the *Old School Hymnal*, first compiled and published in 1920 and now in its twelfth edition, the hymns are numbered. The pages are not.

The original purpose of the foyer was to provide an "air lock," to prevent drafts from entering a fireplace-heated home.

It seems "the shoe is on the other foot" has origins in the 1800s, when each shoe was custom-made for its foot. To wear one's left boot on "the other foot" was especially uncomfortable. How this came to mean karmic retribution is unclear.

Guy Davenport, in a 2002 review of a book by Erich Auerbach, admired that writer's implicit comparison of Odysseus's foot-washing scene and the passage in Virginia Woolf's *To The*

Lighthouse in which Mrs. Ramsay is fitting a wool stocking on her son. "The image rhymes."

Davenport's first book publication was the anonymous 103-page Canadian study guide, *Coles Notes on Homer's The Odyssey*, officially authored by The Coles Editorial Board, published in 1964. His name does appear once, beneath a drawing of two warriors in Classical and Mycenaean armor: "illustrated by the author, Guy Davenport, Ph. D."

The young man enlisted to gain Philoctetes' trust and obtain his magic bow is Neoptolomus, son of Achilles, one of the sailors who originally stranded the ogre on his island.

The Eleanor Wilner poem about Helen Keller is called "Of a Sun She Can Remember."

In "The Open Happens in the Midst of Beings," by Norman Dubie, the speaker has dinner with his wife, his mother-in-law, a psychic hypnotist, and the hypnotist's assistant. There are no deer, but there is an anecdote about an automobile that struck a barn and some cattle.

The Story of My Life was first published in 1903, so Helen Keller was no more than twenty-three when she wrote it. She was not yet eight in late spring 1887, when she had her wellhouse awakening to language.

It is recounted elsewhere that Keller received Miss Sullivan's fingered script of the letters w-a-t-e-r in the same hand over which the well water poured. It was almost certainly Keller's right hand, her nondominant hand. But, from the time she was literate, she read Braille with her left.

Propositionizing is a term coined in the 1870s by English neurologist John Hughlings Jackson to describe constructing in the mind and/or in speech "words or signs referring to one another in a particular manner. Without a proper interrelation of its parts, a verbal utterance would be a mere succession of names, a word-heap, embodying no proposition....The unit of speech is a proposition....Aphasia [is] not only the loss of the power to propositionize aloud (to talk), but to propositionize...internally.... Speech is a part of thought."

Thomas Traherne: "[T]he thought of the World whereby it is enjoyed is better than the World."

Plato is better known than Aristotle for his mistrust of poets.

Sean Lennon has a smaller frame than his stepbrother Julian, but both, like their father, have ectomorphic physiques, and neither is overweight.

Allen Grossman extrapolates his insight about lyric speech from the French linguist Émile Benveniste: "In the social realm human beings look at one another, in the Collective they all look one way. Language is a portal to the collective."

A mirror site is an exact copy of another internet site. A live mirror updates automatically when the original is changed. Pink Roulette is not a mirror, per se; rather, its authors likely took advantage of open source html coding in Man Roulette, which in turn was almost certainly modeled closely after Chat Roulette, a primarily heterosexual speed-dating site.

In *Pilgrim at Tinker Creek*, Dillard wonders at the mental health, not the mental aptitude, of one who stands, on a footbridge, with his back against the onrush. "There must be something wrong with a creekside person who, all things being equal, chooses to face downstream. It's like fouling your own nest. For this and a leather couch they pay fifty dollars an hour?"

Only darker strains of *Agaricus bisporus*, also known as white or button mushroom, are marketed as crimini mushrooms. "White crimini mushroom" is therefore infelicitous. "Crimini white mushroom," on the other hand, in a certain light, is a valid descriptor.

The most direct route from Tucson to St. Louis is 1,483 miles.

In 1980, "Tumbleweed" was the first hit for crossover Country artist Sylvia, best known for her 1982 Country Billboard number one record, "Nobody." Juice Newton never recorded either song.

The tumbleweed diaspore can be a flower cluster of a plant as well as the entire aboveground plant. Species that form tumbleweeds, most common to the amaranth and saltwort families, also exist in the mustard, legume, aster, plantain, and nightshade families in desert and steppe climates. Baby's breath, in its maturity, forms tumbleweeds.

The risk in tickling past the point of pleasure is, for Adam Phillips, the child's "hysteria," "humiliation," and "intensely anguished confusion." He makes no extrapolation from the experience of disarray in being tickled to other corollary fears of uncontainability. But from a comparative study of phobias, he derives a kind of two-degree structure of fear in "First Hates," a later essay in *On Tickling, Kissing, and Being Bored.*

"The tickling narrative, unlike the sex narrative, has no climax." (*Ibid.*)

The term *proprioception* (likewise the term *interoception*) was coined by English neurophysiologist Charles Scott Sherrington, in 1905. Charles Olson, sixty years later, appropriated the word to describe a poetics that appreciates that "movement or action is home" for the person-poet, that personhood has no home "unless the DEPTH implicit in physical being— / built-in space-time specifics and moving (by / movement of 'its own')—is asserted or found- / out as such."

LEAR: What, so young and so untender?
CORDELIA: So young, my lord, and true.
LEAR: Let it be so; thy truth, then, be thy dower…
          …Here I disclaim all my paternal care,
          Propinquity and property of blood
          And as a stranger to my heart and me
          Hold thee, from this, for ever.

Mark Morrisroe was a photographer and performance artist who grew up in Malden, Massachusetts, the son of a drug-addicted mother. He was a prostitute by the age of fifteen and was shot in the chest by a john at seventeen; the bullet remained lodged, too close to the spine to be removed. His photography and performances epitomized the influence of queer punk in the art world in the 1980s and achieved a self-baring radical candor, like that of David Wojnarowicz, especially in his precipitous and fatal illness. He died in 1989.

The Ryan White CARE Act was an August 1990 act of the U.S. Congress to fund a program that would increase availability of care for low-income and uninsured individuals living with HIV or AIDS. Ryan White was an Indiana teenager who was banned from his school after contracting HIV during hemophilia treatment and whose legacy grew from his determination, right up until his death at age eighteen, to reject the discrimination inherent in the term "innocent victim."

By adding the word *asobase* (to play at, to imitate) to any action verb in Japanese, one is softly suggesting the refinement or elite status of the subject performing the act. The honorific additionally acknowledges his or her advanced understanding that ordinary life is only illusion. In Tom Spanbauer's 2001 novel, *In the City of Shy Hunters*, one character, Fiona, teaches the convention of *asobase kotoba* to other characters, who adopt the practice in conversation. "I see you are playing at being a great dancer," says one, and, "I see you are playing at enjoying your Szechuan Chicken."

Fairfield and Anne Porter had James Schuyler as a long-term guest rather than a house sitter, on and off for twelve years, although Schuyler periodically retreated without the Porters to one of their homes, at Great Spruce Head, Long Island. *Freely Espousing*, written during this time, was dedicated to the couple. After Fairfield Porter died, Anne Porter was one of the benefactors who set up a fund that would afford Schuyler a moderately independent home life.

The fuller passage of the 1995 poem "Untitled ['I always put my pussy']" by Eileen Myles is: "I always put my pussy / in the middle of trees / like a waterfall / like a doorway to God / like a flock of birds."

The divot at the top of the sternum between the wings of the collarbone is properly known as the suprasternal notch, or the jugular notch. There is no agreement on a more common, vulgate word for it in English; Germans call it *das Salzfässchen*, or—literally—the salt cellar.

The minutes of a meeting are so called because, as early as the sixteenth century, official record of a meeting was kept in small shorthand script. "Minutes" then derives from the size of the minute notes. The record would be transferred to a document of larger, more legible lettering, for public consumption. That process was called "engrossing."

There is some dispute about Hart Crane's last words. Either Peggy Cowley heard them in the cabin they shared aboard the *Olizaba*: "I have simply been disgraced," or he exclaimed, as some have claimed, at the moment he leapt into the Gulf of Mexico, "Goodbye, everybody!"

Emil Opffer, Sr., exiled anarchist from Holland and longtime editor and publisher of the only Danish-language American newspaper, *Nordlyset*, died in September 1924, seven months after Hart Crane met his son, and more than a year after Crane wrote "Paraphrase." Emil Jr.'s work as a ship's purser took him away from New York on trips that were typically ten days in duration. It was during one of these his father died. *Nordlyset* is Danish for Northern Lights.

Extimacy began in 1995 as a semiannual magazine at University of North Carolina at Chapel Hill. The founding editors, Radha Vatsal and Lisa Stevenson, undergraduates then, were keen to have the journal understood as a flagbearer not of critical theory but of cultural studies, that which existed "in the margins of traditional humanist disciplines" and was not itself "reducible" to a single discipline or practice.

Of the two gay bars on Fifth Avenue in Park Slope Brooklyn in 2005, only Ginger's had a pool table. It was likely the same table that had been in Carrie Nation, a previous incarnation of the bar, at the same address, also gay. It is unclear whether the Carrie Nation referenced in "The Fruit Streets," a poem by Tim Dlugos (1950–90), is the eponymous bar or the temperance activist. If the bar, indications are that it had a previous address in Brooklyn Heights. The poem's newly sober speaker provides a map of sorts for the addressee to find him there.

Striped and solid billiard balls are each six to seven ounces on average, and always a full ounce lighter than the cue ball. Modern tables come with an internal infrastructure of chutes and balances by which the cue ball, if pocketed, is automatically separated out and sent back beneath the table for the next player to place back on the felt and continue the game. This mechanism is called the return.

Lithuanian Jewish philosopher Emmanuel Levinas coined the term *illeity* ("he"-ness) to refer to the ethical limits of address, to "a distance greater than I to Thou." In scholar Bettina Bergo's paraphrase, "Moral height is not expressed in thou-saying; it is a third person relationship."

Macadam is both a nineteenth-century roadmaking technique and a kind of gravel pavement that represented progress in U.S. cities before the widespread use, beginning around 1920, of tar-macadam (or tarmac) and asphalt pavements, which were more suited to motor vehicles. A macadamized road is one in which a stone dust and water mixture has adhered to the surface stones, keeping them in place and protecting the ground beneath. This would have been most common in 1907 Kansas City.

"Confound" derives of the Latin *fundere*, to pour, not *fundus*, meaning bottom. "Foundry" is a cognate. "Fundament" is not.

Satan asks Chaos which way to the light, to a rumored other place not Heaven or Hell, if it exists, and "him thus the Anarch old / with faltering speech and visage incompos'd / answer'd... another world, / hung o'er my realm, link'd in a golden chain / to that side Heav'n whence your legions fell. / If that way be your walk, you have not far; / so much the nearer danger, go and speed; / havoc and spoil and ruin are my gain."

Genesis 11:7. Go to, let us go down and there confound their language, that they may not understand one another's speech.

"I Was Young When I Left Home" is the title given by Bob Dylan to the song that begins with that line. It was recorded in the sessions that produced his 1961 debut eponymous album, but wasn't officially released until 2001 as a bonus track on *Love and Theft*. It is a rendition of a traditional song most often called "Nine Hundred Miles" or "Train 45." Like "Goin' Down Slow," it includes: a letter the speaker either cannot read or cannot write, a call from home, a train that leads home, and resistance to go on account of shameful destitution.

"Abstract relations" constitute the first of the five classes of words in Roget's *Thesaurus*, a classification system which in structure was influenced (like Turing's machines) by Gottfried Leibniz's symbolic thought, itself derivative of Aristotle. Some of Aristotle's *Praedicamenta* are included among Roget's first class of word categories, beginning with 1. Existence.

Valor and Dolor, as such, were not among the gods worshipped in ancient Greece.

In the emerging orthography of the sixteenth century it was custom that every proper name and important common name be cap-

172

italized. Capitalization of personified nouns, names of branches of knowledge, and nouns a writer wished to emphasize became standard practice as well. By the late seventeenth century in England, some printers were capitalizing all nouns, to be on the safe side.

Laura Riding's "Memories of Mortalities" is a long poem in three parts: *My Mother and My Birth, My Father and My Childhood*, and *Sickness and Schooling*. The phrase "the stuttering slow grammaring of self" suggests the work of the first part, while the last part stages an adolescent extension of individuation: "I was apprenticed to my time / And in the craft of contemporaneity / Grew accurate, and by the rule / Of then-and-now I babbled / The abrupt opinion, shuffled / Between what was and is / Like any nonchalant of taught experience." It is with disappointment she recounts that "The child grew girl of current kind."

Leonardo's annotated drawing, usually referred to as *The Vitruvian Man*, was made in 1490, a front view of a standing nude whose limbs are extended at two positions, superimposed. The outstretched arms and legs, in a T position, define the height and width of a rectangle; whereas the spread stance and raised arms (at 5 and 7 o clock, and 10 and 2 o clock), describe the parameter of the body's reach. Vitruvius was an architect who had formulated the proper proportions of a man.

Sandra Blakeslee and her son, Matthew Blakeslee, are the authors of *The Body Has a Mind of Its Own: How Body Maps in Your Brain Help You Do (Almost) Everything Better*. Both are science writers, third- and fourth-generation science writers, in fact, but neither holds a doctorate degree.

About mirror neurons' role in sexual response, the Blakeslees write, "When a man sees two other men in sexual congress, he can't help but experience it…in his mind's body. In effect he feels the 'unnatural' act is being forced on him. Not being gay, he finds the prospect of sex with other men unappetizing."

Steam is water in the gas phase, its evaporation an effect of boiling. When water vapor in cooling atmospheric air reaches dewpoint temperature, it condenses to liquid water, and the effect is called fog—unless it forms on a solid, whereupon it is dew.

Roland Barthes had said that each of his courses at the Collège de France would have at its root a fantasy. His third seminar, after How to Live Together and The Neutral, was called The Preparation of the Novel. It met for the first time in December 1979 but was never completed. Three months later, Barthes was fatally struck by a laundry van as he left campus.

The narrow soft briefcase with interior gusset design for expansion, overtop flap, and front fastener has no consensus name in English. Before the metal-framed box case was popularized in the nineteenth century, such a bag was originally called a budget.

The root of *dossier* is French, /dos/, from the Latin *dorsus*, meaning "back." *Dossier*, in Old French, meant "a bundle of papers labeled on the back."

The *Year-End Countdown* is an annual New Year's Eve special of the syndicated radio program *American Country Countdown*, which, when it began in 1973, played the year's top one hundred hits in Country music. Starting in 1979 this was halved to fifty.

Justice Harry Blackmun co-founded in 1979 and co-moderated for sixteen years the Aspen Institute Seminar on Justice & Society, an annual six-day roundtable discussion, limited to twenty-five invited participants, on how a just society should structure its legal and political institutions.

Painter Joseph Bowler was commissioned in late 1971 by the editors of *Time* magazine for a portrait of President Richard Nixon to reproduce on their January 3, 1972 Man of the Year issue. It was this work (20 inches x 16 inches, oil on Belgian linen) that was rejected for depicting "too sterling a character." The editors had already rejected the epoxy bust of Nixon by sculptor Frank Gallo, the first artist they commissioned. It was that work they found had made "too penetrating a comment." For that reason Bowler was expressly asked to make a "non-committal portrait."

The Collège de France, created in 1530, is neither a university nor a public research center, in traditional senses. It awards no degrees, and its lecture programming is free and open to students without preregistration. At any time there are fifty-two lecture chairs held by fifty-two scholars, who are elected by their peers and who, upon arrival, name their own chairs. Barthes was nominated by Michel Foucault in 1976, and created the chair of literary semiology.

W. H. Auden speculates in a 1969 *New York Review of Books* piece on J. R. Ackerley's memoir *My Father and Myself* about the latter's sexual predilections. Auden later confided to friends that he relished introducing into print the phrase "the Princeton first-year," a euphemism for frottage—on the principle that the particulars of gay sex should not be omitted when relevant in public discourse. "The Princeton rub," and sometimes, more simply, "the Princeton" were also terms in limited use at the time.

An untitled poem by e. e. cummings, which one biographer insists is about his loss of virginity, concludes: "my thumb smashes the world— / frot of furied eyes on brain!heart knotted with A suddenly nakedness"

In the Library of Congress Classification system, work on male homosexuality as such is cataloged in the subclass HQ: The Family, Marriage, Women—under the subrubric Sexual Life. Specifically, HQ 75-76.8. Erotica can be found in the HQ 450s.

Many women and trans men are wary of the overuse and overrepresentation of *scissoring* as a term and a sexual category, especially of its outsize prevalence in cis straight male imagination of the sex that queer women have.

The HIV/AIDS death rate was highest in New York City in 1994; in New York state, 1995.

The first public espousal of the mandate that all HIV-positive gay men should have their status forcibly tattooed on their buttocks came in a widely syndicated March 1986 *New York Times* op-ed by William F. Buckley, Jr: "Identify All the Carriers." It was openly supported by Senator Jesse Helms, but there was no such bill on the floor of either house of Congress.

Welcome to Me (2014, directed by Shira Piven, written by Eliot Laurence) is a comedy about new-age self-involvement and untreated mental illness. The trailer begins with the main character, Alice (Kristin Wiig), putting a tape in the VCR, sitting close, hypnotized. On its spine she has written the words *My True Calling*.

In a 1982 essay, John Berger reports that he and his family had recently driven to Genoa in his Citroën C2V. This is the same model car he reports elsewhere having driven through Yugoslavia during the summer the two erstwhile leaders of Poland and Yugoslavia, Gomulka and Tito, were meeting for the first time, a meeting that took place in 1957. It is likely then that in 1971, when Berger wrote the essay "Field," he drove the Citroën and not a Peugeot.

His essay concludes, "The field you are standing before appears to have the same proportions as your own life."

In late 2010, after the Milltown Dam was destroyed at the west end of the nation's largest Superfund site and the associated reservoir was drained and cleaned of arsenic and heavy metals, the Clark Fork River was no longer diverted and instead channeled into its natural course, toward a confluence again with the Blackfoot River in Bonner, Montana. Migration of fish upstream to the rivers' sources was unimpeded for the first time in 102 years.

Muriel Rukeyser writes, "Remember what happened to you when you came to your poem, any poem whose truth overcame all inertia in you at that moment, so that your slow mortality took its proper place, and before it the light of a new awareness was not something new, but something you *recognized*.

"That is the multiple time-sense in poetry, that is the ever new, which is recognized as something already in ourselves, but not discovered."

In V. I. Propp's *Morphology of the Folktale*, he counts thirty-one functions in the fairy tale; lists and analyzes each; and ascribes them to seven spheres of action, corresponding to their respective performers: 1. the villain, 2. the donor (provider), 3. the helper, 4. the princess or prize and her father, 5. the dispatcher, 6. the hero, and 7. the false hero.

Cutting cocaine refers most commonly to diluting it with adulterants like flour, cornstarch, or powdered milk.

The work that Carrie Meeber (Sister Carrie) first finds in Chicago is in a shoe factory. She punches eyeholes in uppers. She stays with her sister and brother-in-law in their drab flat and repeatedly walks to the foot of the stairs to "stand in the door." When upbraided for it, she claims "I want to see *something*." Charles Drouet, a salesman she meets on a train, is the vehicle for her moral compromise, initiated by his loan to her of "two soft, green, handsome ten-dollar bills." She does not end up in poverty, but rather in fortune as a famous actress.

James Boswell on his "Grand Tour" of Europe, undertaken expressly to meet the "immortal" authors, wrote and presented a letter of introduction of *himself*, by which, in the Swiss village of Môtiers, Jean-Jacques Rousseau was sufficiently intrigued that they met, five times in a fortnight, in December 1764, at the apartment where Rousseau was in exile.

The Armory in lower Manhattan is on Lexington Avenue, between Twenty-Fifth and Twenty-Sixth Streets, a registered landmark. The 69th Infantry Regiment of the New York Army National Guard is stationed there. Throughout the day on September 11, more than eight hundred soldiers from the 69th as well as the 258th and 105th Infantries reported to this location. On September 12, at around 0200, according to Sergeant Major Miguel Cruzado, the soldiers of Company C, of the 105th, a detachment from Jamaica, Queens, were deployed from the Armory to Ground Zero. Their orders were to secure the area of Battery Park.

Early on in Samuel Beckett's *Molloy*, the title character hobbles on a stony lane to catch up with a man about whom he had been speculating—a man with a cigar, a Pomeranian, and a broad stick. Their uneventful exchange there may be called the book's the opening incident. Later, Molloy sleeps the night in the surrounding woods, then "got up, adjusted my crutches and went down to the road, where I found my bicycle (I didn't know I had one) in the same place I must have left it....It was a chainless bicycle, with a free wheel, if such a bicycle exists."

Flowering dogwood is the state tree of Virginia and Missouri only. The state tree of North Carolina is the longleaf pine.

From the years 1858–89, as dated by scientists measuring grease deposits consistent with human habitation in caves where he slept nights, Jules Bourglay, a leatherworker immigrant from France, walked by day, every day, in a continuous circuit of 365 miles, many times over. In her essay "Jules Bourglay, Notable Walker," novelist Samantha Hunt describes his loop as limited to the area east of the Hudson River (opposite side from the Catskills) and west of the Connecticut. He was never married but had been engaged in France to the daughter of the man whose apprentice he was, whose leathercraft business he had inadvertently destroyed in, some say, a lantern fire.

Roger Miller, a novelty singer-songwriter best known for his 1964 hit, "King of the Road," is the singing narrator of the 1973 Disney version of *Robin Hood*, in the role of Allan-A-Dale, the minstrel understood to be one of the Merry Men, animated as a rooster with a lute. Miller was not Appalachia-born, but rather from Erick, Oklahoma, where he grew up farming cotton. Johnny Cash once remarked that Miller's bass voice was closest to his own.

Waylon Jennings was the narrator of *The Dukes of Hazzard* (1979–85), known in the script and credits as The Balladeer. His narration assumed an omniscient vantage and is best remembered for the *entre-nous* teasing remarks and asides to the viewer during freeze-frame cliffhangers at commercial breaks, e.g., "Ain't this fun?"

Jennings, central to the 1970s' "outlaw movement" in Country music, also wrote and performed the show's theme song, "Good Ol' Boys," whose lyrics end with the line "Fightin' the system like a true modern-day Robin Hood." In the show, the Duke boys are said to be former bootleggers sentenced to probation, under which the owning or carrying of firearms was a violation. It is ostensibly for this reason that when Bo and Luke Duke are armed, it is usually with bows and arrows.

Elder Leonard J. Corns (d. 2003) had a radio ministry for thirty-eight years on WHEO AM1670 in Stuart, Virginia, which he recorded separately from the sermons he gave from the pulpit of Old Spoon Creek Primitive Baptist Church in Critz, where he was pastor for fifty years.

James Corner, author of several essays on aerial vantage and the agency of mapping, is prominent in cartographic theory and post-representational cartography but is also well known, internationally famous, as a landscape architect. He was principal designer of The High Line, the elevated greenway and linear park that repurposes the abandoned railway viaduct extending from Gansevoort Street to Thirty-Fourth Street on the West Side of Manhattan.

Three pages into Christopher Isherwood's 1959 novel *Down There On a Visit*, the author-narrator writes, referring to the protagonist Christopher, "now, before I slip back into the convention of calling this young man 'I,' let me consider him a separate being, a stranger almost, setting out on this adventure in a taxi to the docks."

The concluding stanza of "Look Ahead—Look South," the first part of C. S. Giscombe's 1994 book *Here*, reads: "Ohio then, / metaphoric, principled / out past the low gates to school / our clear selves in my memory of school, 3 grades apart / in w/ the other children (some white children always present as well / & big Ohio on the train lines / not the end of the road either but / the destination of chance / —Now why these rueful looks / away, / Sister?"

The cuddly-looking teddy bear cholla cactus has branches that grow in short tubular segments, most commonly called "arms." These segments, once mature, rather easily detach from the entire plant, especially if their bright-sheathed sharp spines catch a passerby.

Gilbert White of Selborne was a "parson-naturalist," that is, a country clergyman who saw the study of natural science as part of his religious work as curate of his parish. His letters about the appearance and behavior of birds, insects, and animals in Selborne, in the county of Southampton, had two addressees: the prominent Welsh zoologist Thomas Pennant and the Hon. Daines Barrington, a barrister in London; but many were never sent. White had been a thoughtful reader of Virgil's *Georgics*, and began at some point to think of the highly observational letters less as correspondence and more as units of his eventual book's form.

The adjectives *this* and *that*, though they are deictic in nature (dependent on a frame of reference), are classified linguistically as demonstratives. *This* is a proximal demonstrative, and *that*, a distal demonstrative. Italian provides a medial demonstrative, referring to objects insufficiently here or there: *codesto*. Its usage is falling out of favor.

Bájate aquí conmigo is the most colloquial way in Spanish to say, "Come down here to me."

Antlers are shed, not molted, annually, by elk and other cervid animals. Shedding is also the term for the procedure by which, once antlers have grown to their maturity, elk scrape away the velvet, which is actually a vascular skin whose tiny blood vessels have nourished antler growth. This latter shedding can be a bloody, protracted event. *Molt* is a word specific to the gradual loss of the winter coat in such animals.

Refractory period is the technical term for the recovery phase after orgasm during which it is physiologically impossible for a man to have another orgasm. It is distinct from a cycle of sexual arousal.

Gilbert White likely observed what became known as a "gossamer shower." The natural phenomenon was perhaps noted earliest by Pliny, who describes a "rain of wool about the Castle Carissa...in the yeare that L. Paulus and C. Marcellus were Consuls" (tr. Philemon Holland, 1601). The sky-fall is in fact silken filaments of spiderwebs, which are first shot at lengths of up to twenty feet from the spinnerets of young spiders, who may then rise and become airborne if a puff of wind takes up the gossamer. A spider can be carried to much higher elevation in this drift, continuing to emit the filaments as a manner of jet propulsion.

Autumn Wreath, Autumn Leaves, Spiced Pumpkin, and Apple Spice are Yankee Candle scents, all in the Fall collection. Autumn

Spice is not a Yankee Candle product. Neither is Clean Towels, as such. Fluffy Towels and Clean Cotton, however, yes, year-round.

Raymond Williams writes, "*Country* as a word derives from *contra* (against, opposite) and has the original sense of land spread out over against the observer. In the thirteenth century it acquired its modern meanings of a tract or region, and of a land or nation."

Kneippism is a form of hydrotherapy which involves walking barefoot through the morning dew.

[acknowledgments]

I would like to thank Mónica de la Torre, Liz Johnston, Nadia Silvassy, Aisha Sabatini Sloan, Emily Cooke, M-C MacPhee, Robert Andrew Perez, Peter Burghardt, Michael Snediker, Paul Vangelisti, Danniel Schoonebeek, John D'Agata, Paul Lisicky, Bradford Morrow, Micaela Morrissette, and Matthew Burgess—editors of the following publications in which these essays first appeared: *BOMB*, *Brick*, *Guernica*, *Harper's*, *NoMorePotlucks*, *Oar*, *The Offing*, *Or: A Literary Tabloid*, the PEN Poetry Series, *The Seneca Review*, *StoryQuarterly*, *Web Conjunctions*, and *Dream Closet: Meditations on Childhood Spaces* (Secretary Press, 2015).

"Correction." was first published as an e-chapbook by Essay Press in 2016. Thanks to Andy Fitch.

Myself is not the single source, not hardly, of what I found I needed to write this book. For their encouragement, advice, and support I am deeply grateful to many.

Above all, John Myers. Who, when it was time, set the tumbleweed free with me.

Stephen Motika, for believing in the project of the book.

Emery Jones, for believing in the greater project.
Mirto Stone, who asked for a better opposite of expert.

Maggie Nelson. Chris Nealon. Jason Zuzga. Karen Brennan. Boyer Rickel. At every step.

Samuel Ace, Beth Alvarado, Brett Bell, Matthew Burgess, Justin Cavin, Barbara Cully, Hannah Ensor, Jesse Aron Green, Annie Guthrie, Annie Gwynne-Vaughan, Jacob Kahn, Aaron Kunin, Farid Matuk, Vestal McIntyre, Molly McKasson, Jane Miller, Robert E. Moore, Eileen Myles, Mary Jane Nealon, Lou Pepe, John Pluecker, Claudia Rankine, Allan Reeder, Ben Rutherfurd, Prageeta Sharma, Richard Siken, Aisha Sloan, Doug Stockstill, TC Tolbert, Matias Viegener, Jacqueline Waters, Ken White: thank you.

And to Mary Austin Speaker, Justin Hargett, Lindsey Boldt, and Anne Cherry: I'm indebted to your artistry, effort, and know-how.

My great gratitude, finally, to the George A. and Eliza Gardner Howard Foundation for its generous support.

In loving memory of Irene Lawson Overby (1928-2014).
In loving memory of Jeremy Isajiw (1978-2014).

[nightboat books]

Nightboat Books, a nonprofit organization, seeks to develop audiences for writers whose work resists convention and transcends boundaries. We publish books rich with poignancy, intelligence, and risk. Please visit nightboat.org to learn more about us and how you can support our future publications.

The following individuals have supported the publication of this book. We thank them for their generosity and commitment to the mission of Nightboat Books:

Elizabeth Motika

Benjamin Taylor

In addition, this book has been made possible, in part, by grants from the National Endowment for the Arts and the New York State Council on the Arts Literature Program.